Table of Contents

Foreword	1
Introduction	3
Before You Leave: The Pre-Call Prep	7
Stop 1: Introduce Yourself	27
Road Block: Nobody is at the First Stop	41
Stop 2: Rapport Building	51
Stop 3: Discovering a Need	75
Stop 4: The Pitch	93
Stop 5: The Close	141

Road Block: Objections	165
Dead End: "No"	197
Final Destination: Closed Sale	205
A Note from Jason	215
Sources Noted	217

Your Road Map to Success in Sales

A Step-by-Step Guide to Closing Your Next Sales Call

Jason Karaman, MBA

Foreword by Anthony Iannarino, author of *The Only Sales Guide You'll Ever Need* and *The Lost Art of Closing: Winning the 10 Commitments That Drive Sales*

Copyright © 2017 by Jason Karaman

All rights reserved. This book or any portion thereof may not be reproduced or used in any manner whatsoever without the express written permission of the publisher and author except for the use of brief quotations in a book review.

This publication is designed to provide accurate and authoritative information in regard to the subject matter covered. It is sold with the understanding that the publisher and author are not engaged in rendering legal, accounting, or other professional service.

Printed in the United States of America

Cover design by Top Book Designer

ISBN-13: 978-1976411748

ISBN-10: 1976411742

First Edition, 2017

Foreword

By Anthony Iannarino, founder of *The Sales Blog* and author of *The Only Sales Guide You'll Ever Need* and *The Lost Art of Closing: Winning the 10 Commitments That Drive Sales*

There isn't any more valuable use of your time as a salesperson than the time you spend face-to-face with your prospective clients. It's difficult to gain the time for a first meeting, and because your prospective clients are busier than ever, the time you get is often too short, too rushed, and too valuable to waste.

Why then don't we prepare to make those interactions as meaningful and valuable as they need to be? Why do we assume that because we have made hundreds or thousands of sales calls, that we are using this time to maximum effect? K. Anders Ericsson, the expert on expertise once wrote, "I have been walking for 48 years, but I don't believe I am getting any better at it." Because we have repeatedly done something does not mean that we are improving, and it doesn't indicate that we are doing it as well as we might think.

To my knowledge, and I have read countless books on sales, this is the very first book of its kind; a whole treatise on sales calls. It is a book that is long overdue, and one that needed to be written. If there is a critical aspect to selling well, what could be more important to success or failure than the actual sales calls we make? If success is not found here, if this isn't where the preference for you and your solution is created, I defy you to tell me where these things are found.

Enter *Your Road Map to Success in Sales.* Jason Karaman, in a carefully crafted treatment of sales calls, provides you with the guidance you need to perform better when you are face to face with your clients (or ear to ear, for that matter). In five major stops along this journey, you find a plan for introducing yourself, building rapport, discovering needs, pitching your prospect (an idea that causes some great consternation and one that I love and agree with), and the close (or making for commitments, in my vernacular).

A sales call, like a sales process, can easily go nonlinear because of the great variability in the complex, human dynamic that is a conversation. Not to worry, along each stop, your author will help you address the road blocks on your way to your final destination.

It is important that you read this book. It is more important that take action to improve your performance during each and every sales interaction. The mark of a true professional is the willingness to retain the beginner's mind. Even if you have made a thousand sales calls, I promise your next call will be massively improved after reading this book.

Introduction

"Sales success comes after you've stretched yourself past your limits on a daily basis" – Omar Periu, self-made multimillionaire businessman

---

If you've picked this book up, you might be considering a new career in sales, just accepted your first sales position, or you are an experienced representative who wants to get back to the basics.

You might also be in one of the dozens of other professions that requires you to win somebody over to your way of thinking, such as education, law, medicine, or coaching.

Whether you want to believe it or not, everything we do essentially boils down to sales. If you work in business you have to constantly be selling your product, service, or ideas to people. If you work in law you have to sell your arguments to people. If you work as a writer or artist you have to sell your creative thinking and your abilities. If you are an educator you have to sell the value in the material that you are teaching. No matter what you might do professionally you can be sure that at some point, you're going to have to convince someone to do something or win them over to your thought processes.

Convincing somebody to do something that they would have not normally done is a pretty difficult thing to accomplish. It requires the convincing party to fundamentally change the mind of their audience in such a way where both parties appear to be better off. It requires both parties to come to a mutual conclusion in which they are both satisfied. I would make the argument that this is one of the most difficult things to accomplish because people inherently dislike change, no matter how beneficial it may seem. Selling a product or service to a potential customer is one of the most challenging yet rewarding experiences that you can have in the business world. There is a reason why it is called the "thrill of the sale."

Those who work in business, particularly those who work in sales or marketing, have to perform this incredible task on a daily basis. Not only that, their livelihood depends on how well they can do it. Those who are good at it can do very well financially, while those who are challenged by it usually do not make it in that career path.

The possibility of failure is a stressful idea for salespeople. Most of them have minimum quotas that they must hit, or else they will be fired and replaced. Employers are in the business of making a profit, not giving away free money. Therefore, as a salesperson, you have to be able to perform at optimal levels to even keep your job. If you want to make some real money, you have to be even better than that.

That's why salespeople are always constantly looking for ways they can improve their game. It does not matter if you are just starting out or if you have been in sales for the past two decades. It's important to open your mind and to gain different perspectives on the sales process.

Ruts usually happen when a salesperson goes "stale" and gets in a bad rhythm. Only the ones who have committed to a policy of constantly improving will successfully get out of the sales slump and will come back stronger than before.

The process presented here in this book is one that I created during my first sales job. I was a recent college graduate of Purdue University and was determined to succeed professionally in the world of sales and marketing. Soon after graduation I accepted a position doing outside sales for a manufacturing company in Atlanta, Georgia. At the time, I wanted to be a strong salesperson so badly that I devoted much of my efforts to learning the sales process and gathering as much help as possible from different books, blogs, Podcasts, etc. I wanted to create a process that worked for me. It had to be effective yet creative and easy to remember.

By the time I had actually started working, I had created out my own "Sales Road Map" with several various stops. Each "stop" representing a step in the sales process. The final destination, of course, is a closed sale.

Being that I was so young and inexperienced I made a lot of mistakes along the way. Trial and error sometimes is one of the best teachers in life and it certainly taught me a thing or two about the world of business. Therefore, the process evolved over a period of a few years until I was finally able to make it work for me.

This is just one process out of dozens that already exist. I'm not saying that this is the absolute best one to use, but it did allow for me, as a rookie 21 year old salesperson right out of college, to grow my territory at a significantly higher rate than was expected.

After that first sales position I accepted a role doing inside sales at a different company. Rather than knocking on doors all day, I spent my time behind a computer quoting prices to various construction companies. Using the same process I was able to exceed my goals and became one of the top performers at that company.

This book was designed to help people through the sales process in the same easy to understand format that I used early on in my career. Not surprisingly, I still use this process because it works so well. This material is designed primarily for those who are beginning their career in sales, but those who are experienced and are looking to get back to the basics will find this valuable as well.

People sometimes make sales to be more complicated than it needs to be. This process will lay out five steps in a format where you can easily recall it and use it in the real world. Each step will allow you to procedurally go through a sales call without 'shooting from the hip.' By adhering to this method, you will eventually be able to handle anything that comes your way and will be able to see success at the end of your sales calls. It does not matter if you sell over the telephone or if you sell in a face-to-face setting. This road map can be used in either circumstance.

By design, this book itself is relatively short for the scope of material being covered. I wanted to make it easy to read, easy to understand, and quick to apply. You should be able to read this book and apply the methods presented here to your job immediately. People tend to complicate the sales cycle – this book is meant to show you that it can be implemented easily and can reflect positive changes as early as your next paycheck.

Thank you for taking the time to read this! I really hope you all see the same results as I have with this process. I'd like to take a brief moment and give a simple shout-out to my wife, Ashley. Without her support and her advice, this book would not be possible.

I also would like to extend a huge thank you to everybody who contributed to the editing process of this book: Ashley Karaman, Brandon Brassard, Dr. Clark Trask, and the folks at Grammarly.

Before You Leave: The Pre-Call Prep

"The journey of a thousand miles begins with one step." – Lao Tzu, ancient Chinese writer and founder of philosophical Taoism

Figure out your why

The absolute first thing that you will want to do ironically has nothing to do with the sales process at all. It has nothing to do with sales knowledge, business models, product knowledge, competition analysis, or marketing mix. Essentially, this has nothing to do with business at all. Yet, if we do not do this, we might be dooming ourselves before we even start to think about going on a sales call. At the very minimum, failing to do this will result in work that is either done grudgingly or done with minimal effort. Before we even decide that we are going to be selling anything, it is imperative that we figure out and define our *why*.

In our sense, a "why" can be defined as a reason for something to be existing or a reason why an action is being performed. Some people spend entire philosophical careers wondering what the reason for existence is by asking the fundamental question "why are we here?" It's a profound concept that makes us human. As children, we are constantly asking "why?" when our parents tell us to do something. It's not that we are being snarky or disobedient - we are just trying to figure out a reason for the action. Without having a well-defined *why*, it can be difficult to fully commit to something.

The same can be said about working in sales, marketing, business, or honestly, any profession that requires a significant amount of your time and your energy. For the purpose of sales, we should be defining two primary *whys* before we set off on our road trip: our *personal why*, and our *professional why*.

Define your personal why

Our *personal why* comes before our *professional why* because, in my opinion, it's a more powerful concept and can sometimes be the defining factor in personal success, regardless of what you do professionally.

Your *personal why* can be defined as your reason for getting out of bed in the morning and going to work. It's the thing that makes you tick and drives you to succeed.

It's an easy definition to type out, and an even easier concept to understand at face value. However, actually defining your own *personal why* requires some deep introspection and some honest personal soul-searching.

I had a gentleman tell me that his *personal why* for getting out of bed and going to work every day was to make money. We all work in sales, which is a very results and profit-driven industry to work in. Most people want to work in sales to make as much money as possible. There is nothing wrong with that, but that is not a *personal why*. Making a bunch of money is simply a result from working - it's not the reason why you work so hard and devote so much of your life to work. Your *personal why* needs to be much deeper than that.

Several months ago, I was having lunch with a top performing sales representative and we were discussing this concept. For the sake of privacy, I'll omit his name, but he had one of the best *personal whys* I had ever heard. He told me that his wife had grown up in extreme poverty in Kentucky. She had, quite literally, nothing that a normal kid growing up should have had. No Christmas presents, no birthday parties, no clean clothes, etc. When he married her, he made a vow that he would work to give her the life that she deserves. He vowed that he would work as hard as he could to make sure that she had nice things and had those luxuries that most people take for granted. He wakes up and goes to work every day with her in mind. If he sells, it's not for personal reasons…it's to provide her a good life. If he does not sell, he let her down.

That's a strong *personal why*. That's the sort of *personal why* that gives him the capability to be a top performing sales executive, regardless of external factors. It gives him the drive to come to his job every day, work harder than the rest, master his craft, and close more deals. No matter what, he will do whatever he can to provide her with that life. He will never lose and will always be a top performer.

Like I said, that's one of the most powerful *personal whys* I had ever heard before. You might not have a *why* that is similar to that. Perhaps your why is that you want to send your child to college. Maybe it's that you want to travel the world. Perhaps it's that you want to give as much back in the form of charity as you can. Or maybe your why is that you have a deep desire to win and be the best salesperson at your company. Truth be told, it does not matter what exactly your *personal why* is. If it's your own *personal why*, it's important to you. If it's truly important to you, use it for motivation. Never forget it. Write it down and keep it in a place where you will always see it. Use it to win.

Someone who has a *personal why* that is truly important to them will be an unstoppable force. In sales, your *why* will help you out of ruts and will help you push through failure. It will force you to want to improve and get better each and every day. Remembering your *why* will prevent you from slacking off and wasting time. It will cause you to rise above and win.

Defining your *personal why* before you embark on your sales call and your entire mindset will be different. It will be less of "I hope I get this sale" and more of "I WILL get this sale." As we will explore later on in this book, your mindset and general attitude can make all the difference.

Know your professional why

Once you define your *personal why*, you can take a look at the company that you work or the product that you sell and identify the *why* behind that.

Using similar terminology, the *professional why* can be defined as the reason for a company or a product to exist. Again, the reason why a company exists is not to make money. That's merely a result of the company doing their daily activities. Similar to the *personal why*, a company/product has to have a strong *why* behind it that fuels their motivation.

A good way to figure out your *professional why* is to look at the mission statement of your company. Each company has a well-defined mission statement that serves to drive and motivate the individuals within that company.

Coca-Cola, one of the world's leading beverage companies, has a well-defined and powerful mission statement that every employee stands behind. Their mission statement is "To refresh the world in mind, body and spirit. To inspire moments of optimism and happiness through our brands and actions."[1] Notice that nowhere in there it says that making money is their primary goal - it's just the result of the execution of their mission. You can see their mission statement come to fruition in everything that they do, from their advertisements to their worldwide distribution network.

Every company has a mission statement. Figure out what yours is and take it to heart. Having a shared vision and a shared set of values and goals is important because it not only helps build trust with prospects, but helps you trust the company that you work for. We will dive into this later on, but showing a strong and unified front to the prospect is important in building trust. Sharing the same set of core values and a shared mission only enhances the chance of establishing trust.

Another way you can define your *professional why* is to have a passion for what you sell and have that clearly identified in your head. For example - you might sell houses because you have a true passion for helping people find their dream home. I have actually spoken to and worked with many funeral professionals who could care less about the money because they have a real passion for helping families get through their toughest hours. If you have a true and real passion for what you do professionally, that can serve as a very powerful *professional why* too.

Finding your *why*, both personally and professionally can be challenging. You might have to do some deep introspection before you figure it out. Even if you do figure it out, it's easy to lose sight of it. Every now and again, it's imperative that you take a time out to figure out what your *whys* are so you can not only gain a fresh perspective, but a regained motivation to succeed.

Know your sales steps

After we figure out what our *whys* are, we can begin to prepare for our trip. As with a real road trip, we need to make sure everything is good with our itinerary before we leave. Like most trips you'll want to know where you are going and what stops you need to make ahead of time. After all, you would not just embark on a trip with a set destination without consulting a map first. The same logic applies here. Your final destination is a closed sale, your "map" is your sales presentation, and your stops are the steps within the sales cycle.

Knowing all this information ahead of time is crucial to a successful sales call. It allows you to strategize and think about how you can most effectively make a sale. Going in to present a sales pitch after you have rehearsed and memorized it is far easier than simply winging it.

In this case, we have five different stops that are required on our road map to a closed sale. Each stop is listed as the following:

1. Introduce Yourself
2. Rapport Building
3. Discovering a Need
4. The Pitch
5. The Close

Your final destination is, of course, a closed sale. During our road trip there will be several potential road blocks that we will have to overcome. These will be addressed at the time they are encountered, but they are worth noting here so when we encounter one, we can recognize it.

1. There is No Prospect to Pitch
2. Prospect Says "No"

We will go over how to get past these road blocks later on. For now, we will only focus on the stops and how to prepare you for the trip.

<u>Don't look for shortcuts</u>

When looking at an actual map, the first thing that most people do is look for shortcuts that will help them reach their destination faster. I know that I want to shorten my commute as much as possible, so I'm definitely guilty of that as well. The problem arises when something goes wrong. Taking a shortcut might get you to where you are going more quickly, but you might end up turned around and lost. Prior to GPS this was a common occurrence; nevertheless the analogy fits perfectly with our sales road map as well.

If you try to skip one of the steps of the sales cycle, you might close a sale. It's entirely possible that you can close sales by skipping multiple steps as well. However, more often than not, you'll end up lost in your own presentation which gives the prospect complete control of the conversation.

Another reason why you should make sure that you complete every step is that the steps build upon each other. Skipping a step will render the next one less effective and will weaken your overall presentation.

This road map was designed to be a one-size-fits-all approach to any prospect or any customer. It did not matter if I was in a face-to-face setting or if I was selling over the phone, I never had to alter the steps. By adhering to the road map, I found that I closed much more frequently than those times where I tried to take shortcuts.

Imagine that you are taking a historical tour through Europe, where every stop contains important historical information about the continent, with each stop building upon the one previous. Skipping stops might ruin the experience and might cause you to be less appreciative. The steps in our cycle are designed to build value up to the customer, leading to a closed sale. Skipping steps only means that you have less time to build value. In sales, value is everything.

Prepare your strategy

It's important to know your destination and where you have to stop. The best approach is to have a strategy and a plan of action. That's why it's important to prepare yourself ahead of time.

Your strategy can be compared to your vehicle. This is the tool that you will use to get from your starting point to the finish line. You have to make sure that your car is in perfect working order and you have everything fine-tuned before you leave.

This is where gathering information is important. You should obtain as much pertinent information about your prospect as possible. However, this can be a slippery slope. If you gather too much information you can easily start to rationalize why the prospect will not purchase. If you start to go down that road, you've *already* lost the sale before you've even spoken to your prospect. Gathering too little information can also be a detriment if hit with unexpected information that you had not prepared for.

That's why we will employ a pre-call routine that is appropriately named the *C.A.L.L. Strategy.*

C.A.L.L. is a simple acronym. Each letter represents a component of the pre-call process. This process enables you to gather the correct amount of information to gain a sale. No more, no less. The letters themselves stand for:

Create similarity
Analyze the facts
Leverage yourself
Leave your judgment outside

Consider this as the gasoline for your car. Fill your tank with all the important information and you will go far. If you only fill it halfway, you're in trouble.

This strategy is very helpful for those who have the chance to look at their client information ahead of time. If you are cold calling or pitching to someone without any information, these steps can still be completed ahead of time by knowing your different customer 'clusters' and your overall general strategy for each group.

For example, let's say that you are working as a car salesperson. For the sake of simplicity, let's say that you sell two types of cars - luxury 2-door models and family-style 4-door models. While you cannot possibly know ahead of time who fits the bill for a 2-door or a 4-door when they walk in, you can generalize ahead of time who the target market is for each model and customize your pitch to each style of customer. It's all about knowing your product inside-and-out and how to pitch it to each individual.

Bear in mind that this strategy is assumptive by nature. You'll notice that a lot of the contents in the strategy involve either doing research on a lead or making certain assumptions. This can be really helpful in determining what your overall strategy will be, but you should also be aware that it's not perfect. Customers occasionally will throw out random facts and ideas that conflict with your assumptions. That's OK – more often than not, this model can be effectively used and can be relied upon. A top performer has the ability to think on his or her feet and is able to switch gears if something unexpected happens down the road.

For the remainder of the section (and this book) we will pretend that you are a newly trained home security salesperson. You were just hired at the Safe Security Company* and were assigned to work a territory in northern Atlanta, Georgia. You will be knocking on doors to get the majority of your business, but will occasionally attempt to close some deals over the phone as well.

*Names, characters, businesses, places, products, events and incidents are either the products of my imagination or used in a fictitious manner. Unless otherwise stated, any resemblance to actual persons (living or dead), businesses, and actual events is purely coincidental.

C – Create similarity

The first thing you should look to do is to create similarity around the customer. This means a couple different things:

- You should search for common ground between the prospect and your current customers.
- You should search for similarities between you and the prospect.

The first benefit in doing this is that if you are able to see a similarity between the client and some of your existing customers, it will make it easier for you to discover a similar need. By anticipating what the customer might want, you will be able to be more efficient in your questioning. Also, this will give you the chance to anticipate any objections that the client might give you. If you have already closed on prospects with similar problems and objections, you will be more confident in your presentation and will be more mentally prepared.

The second benefit is that you can use true third party stories during your presentation. People like hearing relatable examples. The third party story remains one of the best tools to use during your pitch. We will go into that more later on, but being able to recognize that you have relatable examples will help you tremendously down the road.

The final benefit is that you will gain some good talking points during the rapport building phase. I believe that it's an important part of the process to create similarity with the prospect on a personal level. Whether it's talking about their favorite sports team or discussing their family – having this information ahead of time will ensure a smooth rapport building process. We will go over the details of rapport building later on during stop 2.

A – Analyze the facts

Facts in themselves are not dangerous – they are actually one of the most helpful tools that you can have in your sales kit. When facts suddenly become opinions you start to slip down the slope of judgment, which is one of the worst things that can happen in this business. You have to separate out the facts from the opinions.

The best way to separate out the facts from the opinions is to look at the basic information surrounding a lead. Where are they from? What kind of business are they in? Who is their current supplier? How much are they being charged? All of these examples contain information that is relevant to the next step, which is actually leveraging you for a sale.

It's important to note here that you should not use this information to mentally psych yourself out. It's incredibly easy to look at a lead and say "Well, they are already buying from XYZ Home Security, which has FAR better prices than I can offer, so what's the point in even trying?" Working in sales is tough enough as it is – don't end the road trip before you even leave.

So, as the newly trained representative for the Safe Security Company, you survey the houses that you will be calling upon and notice that one house already has coverage with XYZ Home Security (you can see the security sign planted in their front yard), while the other house does not appear to have anything.

L – Leverage yourself

Leveraging yourself for a sale means selecting a specific area to focus on when presenting your product or service. Essentially, this is the step where you want to pick a general strategy based on the facts that you uncovered in the previous step.

Going back to the security example, you will want to formulate a strategy (or an 'angle') for each scenario: one strategy for the house with the competition and one strategy for the house with no service. For the house with coverage already, you can leverage yourself with the fact that the competitor does not offer live emergency video monitoring with security cameras, while yours does. This will be one of your selling points when pitching to the prospective customer.

In terms of the other house with no coverage, you can leverage yourself with the knowledge that there has been a rise in the level of breaks-ins recently.

This step takes a little bit of legwork on your side with knowing your competition and your product environment. It's well worth your time to study not only your own company and your own product, but what the competition is up to as well.

Leveraging yourself does not mean that you should pigeonhole yourself to one single strategy. It means that you should have a few different selling points that you will want to communicate to the customer. Knowing this ahead of time will allow for a smoother pitch and will show the customer that you know what you are talking about.

This step is so crucial because it will allow you to enter the sales pitch with greater confidence too. Rather than scrambling for selling points, you will have a few already picked out and ready to go. To properly leverage yourself, make sure you know your product/service inside and out. Again, you also have to dive deep into your industry and what your competition is up to.

This will require substantial time on your part, but will make all the difference in the world. Most companies will offer training in some form or another about the features and benefits of your product compared to the competition, so be sure to take notes and study them in your free time. Studying your craft on your own time is what separates the top performers from those who merely scrape by.

L- Leave your judgment at the door

One of the most dangerous things about the previous three steps (particularly the *Analyze the Facts* step) is that it's incredibly easy to form biased opinions based on your research. If you start to pre-judge a prospect before even shaking their hand or speaking with them, you might be severely hurting your process.

Going back to the security example - let's say that you are looking at the house without service and see a couple of broken down cars parked in the driveway. Next door at the house with current service, you see a brand new $60,000 car.

It is way too easy to look at the house with the broken down cars and assume that they will not have the money to afford your premium security services, while the house with the nice car definitely will. You decide to forgo the house with the old cars completely.

These are very dangerous opinions. What if the house with the nice car is in tremendous debt and is filing for bankruptcy tomorrow, while the house with the older cars has zero debt and a bunch of liquid cash? You just lost a potential sale.

These are facts that you cannot know ahead of time. Forming opinions based on what you see can lead to missed opportunities.

Even worse, what if you pitch to the house with the old cars and rush through the entire thing because you believe in your head that they cannot even afford it? You'll self-sabotage yourself and will surely lose out on a sale.

While this may seem easy, leaving your judgment at the door can be one of the most difficult lessons to apply in sales. It's human nature to judge others. I have had many people tell me that one of their favorite activities is to people watch because it's fun to judge others. It's practically built into our DNA. Working in sales you have to overcome that and treat every single person as a prospective buyer, whether they drive a $100,000 car or a $500 car.

Check your attitude

Attitude is probably one of the most important elements in all of sales. If you have a bad attitude before you even present the product or service, you are almost guaranteeing that you will not get a sale.

If we return to the analogy that your strategy is the vehicle that you will use to get from here to your destination, your positive attitude is the oil that runs the car. It's the lifeblood of your car. Failing to put oil in the car and you can forget about even reaching your first stop.

Zig Ziglar, master salesman and one of the most influential sales trainers once said "Your business is never really good or bad 'out there.' Your business is either good or bad right between your own two ears." [2]

Everybody goes through periods where they have bad attitudes. Much like everything else, it's a human trait to have. We are not robots – when people say "no," it feels *bad*. After hearing "no" several times in a row, it can really have a negative impact on our mental state. If you carry this weight with you during your next sales call, it will certainly have a negative impact on your overall sales presentation.

This is where being emotionally intelligent and being mentally tough come into play.

Emotional intelligence

You don't need a PhD in Psychology to understand emotional intelligence. Essentially, *emotional intelligence* is just a fancy phrase for being able to tell when you are angry, sad, happy, etc. While the concept is simple (we all can pretty easily tell when we are happy or sad), actually doing something about it is the challenging part.

Part of having emotional intelligence is having the ability to change your emotions based on your environment.

Imagine that you are an actor on a stage. It's opening night and the theater is sold out. Right in the front row are some critics from the local newspaper. The audience (critics especially) quite frankly do not care what is going on in your personal life. They are there to see a show! It's your job to check your attitude back stage and perform for your audience.

Working in sales is no different. If you want to capture the attention of your prospect, you have to be able to fight past your bad attitude. You have to be able to withstand all the negatives that life throws at you and put on a great show for your prospect. Most people call this *mental toughness.*

<u>Mental toughness</u>

There is nothing easy about working in the business world. It's a stressful and challenging career path to choose. It does not matter if you are working at a massive publicly held manufacturing company, or working at a small technology startup – there will always be one thing that unites all those who work in sales…*it's hard.*

Mental toughness is what separates those who give up 8 months in from those who spend decades in the industry. It's what separates those who wake up and dread going to work from those who are excited to start the day. Ultimately, it's what separates those who are successful from those who are not.

There are five main components to being mentally tough. Those components are ambition, improvement, flexibility, competitiveness, and heart.

Ambition gives you the aspect of forward-thinking. If you have a goal in mind and have the internal drive to achieve that goal, nothing will stop you. Let's say that your goal is to sell the most security coverage that a rookie has ever done in the history of the company. That's a pretty intense goal, but if you are ambitious enough to set that goal and if you really want to achieve it, you will withstand anything to make it happen.

Subscribing to a philosophy of non-stop self-improvement will give you the opportunity to learn from your failures and turn them into positive experiences, rather than detrimental disasters. We all fail at some point. It will happen to you. Perhaps you have a bad first year and don't even come close to being the top performing rookie that you were hoping for. Learning from your mistakes and your experiences will be the difference between a potentially record-breaking second year or becoming burnt out and quitting.

Flexibility will allow for you to cope with change. Our world is ever changing and the realm of sales is not immune to that. The rise of technology and the sociological movements of cultures are rapidly evolving on a daily basis. Staying informed and remaining on the cutting edge of these changes will allow you to adapt more comfortably. If you are able to handle change and be flexible with your preconceived notions, you'll be able to seek out the benefits of change rather than the negatives.

Finally, having the heart (or a passion) for what you do can make all the difference in the world. Nobody was ever able to withstand the pressures of something without having a deep desire to do what they do. Find something that you are passionate about – you'll be able to go further than you ever thought. Your passion can be anything. It can be a passion for your product, service, or industry. It can be a passion for winning. It can even be a passion for sales itself. Whatever it is, make sure you know it and remember it. Your 'why' should feed your passion.

It's important to look at yourself in the mirror to determine if you have all of these elements. If you do not, work on incorporating them into your mental state. Your success ultimately depends on it.

Final check

Alright, so far, we have our road map in hand, which lays out the five stops that are necessary for our road trip. This will ensure that we do not get lost along the way. We are also aware that there are two major road blocks that we have to watch out for.

We have two houses that we can sell our product to - house A and house B. House A has coverage with our competition, while house B has no coverage. We decide that house A is a good candidate for pitching our live video-monitoring service to because the competition does not offer this service. We also decide that house B is a good candidate because the rise of crime rates and break-ins in the area mean that they certainly need protection. We have our vehicle (our strategy) filled with gasoline (the information about the prospect). The tank needs to be 100% full to reach our final destination, so do a final check to make sure that our gauge is on F. Finally, we completed an oil change to remove our bad, dirty attitude and replaced it with a good, clean attitude.

We are finally ready to start on our journey to the final destination: a closed sale. Let's go!

Stop 1: Introduce Yourself

"The handshake of the host affects the taste of the roast" – Benjamin Franklin, polymath and Founding Father of the United States

---

Our first stop is called *Introduce Yourself*. Some people might call it the *Introduction* or the *Greeting* step. Although this is only the first stop in our journey (and the shortest), some would call it the most important one.

They say that people form opinions on you based on the first few seconds. If someone forms a positive opinion of you during this step, you will have a much easier time down the road. If someone forms a negative opinion of you, the rest of your journey will be an uphill battle.

Have you ever taken an actual road trip where the first stop was terribly disappointing? It ruins the experience for the rest of the trip and makes you wonder if the road trip will be worth it. The first stop has to exceed expectations. You have to start your trip off with a bang.

The fact of the matter is that people buy from those that they like. We will dig more into this during a later stop, but this introduction step lays the foundation for that principle. A proper introduction will start your sales presentation off with a bang and will leave the prospect wanting more.

Saying hello

What's in a "hello?" Well, quite a bit, actually.

The way that we start off our conversation can be compared to dropping a rock into a pond. If you drop a pebble, it will create a small ripple effect. If you drop a huge stone, the ripple effect will be more pronounced and will go on for much longer. The same logic applies here.

If you start off your conversation with a meek and quiet "Hi, how are ya?" you'll hardly make an impact on the prospect. This is where you want to gain the attention of the prospect and where you want to establish command.

Your 'hello' phrase should have a few different components in it. You should accomplish three primary things during this step:

1. Gain the attention of your audience
2. Clearly introduce yourself
3. Establish command of the conversation

If you are able to accomplish these three things during this stop, the rest of the journey will be much easier because you will have an audience who is engaged and who is interested in what will happen next.

Gain the attention of your audience

The best way to gain the attention of your prospect is to be cheerful and engaged. In essence, you want to show a certain level of excitability in your pitch. Put yourself in their shoes – if you are learning about a product from someone who obviously does not want to be there and isn't excited about anything, why would you want to buy it from them? In fact, why would you even listen to them in the first place?

If you are unable to gain the attention of the prospect right off the bat, you'll be fighting an uphill battle trying to gain their attention later on. An easy way to gain their attention is to utilize the 3 E's – **Energy, Excitement, and Enthusiasm**.

The concept of the 3 E's is not a new one. It's been utilized in many different scenarios ranging from associate/employee engagement to helping people with Autism. It's a concept that is tried and true for grabbing the attention of your audience and focusing them on what you are saying. This can be a huge win for you in sales if you are able to master each element.

Lucky for us, they are not that difficult to understand or master. With a little bit of practice, you should be able to easily engage your prospect and have them hanging on every word that you say.

Energy

Energy is easily communicated. It's probably one of the easiest of the three to master, because it has relatively little to do with what you say or how you say it. Sure, you can communicate energy through your tone of voice and verbiage, but that's more so tied in with excitement and enthusiasm. Where prospects really see your energy is in your non-verbal body language.

Somebody once told me that body language constitutes over half of communication alone. You want to be communicating an energized message with your body language, which will make the customer feel energized as well. In psychology, mirroring is where people (in this case, your prospect) will subconsciously imitate your body language. Wouldn't you rather have customers who are positive and fun too?

Communicating energy through body language can be achieved through good posture, appropriately timed hand-gestures, smiling, eye contact, head nodding, active listening, laughing, and a good, strong handshake. Fighting the urge to yawn is crucial here too. If you do all the above, your customer should feel your energy and it should get them energized too, making them more receptive to hearing your pitch.

When someone walks through the door or when you meet someone, give a big smile, extend your hand, and make direct eye contact.

If you are on the phone, this is a little more difficult to accomplish, but you should still communicate a high level of energy by smiling, even if nobody is there to see it. Prospects can often 'hear' the smile in the tone of your voice. This is why many top performing salespeople have mirrors in their offices/cubicles. They want to ensure that they are smiling when talking to prospects. Sit up straight in your chair and have a pen & paper ready to take notes. You'll be surprised at how subtle the effect is, yet how impactful it can be.

Excitement

Excitement is found in the tone of your voice. Having a higher tone during crucial moments communicates a level of excitement that cannot be found in a monotone pitch.

Think about one of your old teachers or professors who spoke in a very monotone voice. Everybody has experienced at least one instructor like this. Odds are you were bored and not engaged, so you zoned out and missed the content.

Now think about one of your old teachers or a professor who was always excited and was always speaking in a dramatic fashion. I doubt that you were playing around with your phone and ignoring the material. You were probably engaged and interested in what he/she was saying. The same logic applies here too!

It's also worth noting that excitement can be communicated by the loudness of your voice. Of course, you shouldn't be screaming in the customer's face or in the receiver of your phone, but you definitely do not want the prospect straining to hear what you have to say.

Writing about tone of voice is extremely difficult because it's hard to put into words how to change it, but one of my managers had some great advice for me when I was having trouble. As top performing salesperson and skilled performance juggler who knew how to command audiences, he said "Try to be a caricature of yourself," meaning that I should amplify the traits that I was trying to communicate. Of all the advice and science that's out there to help with tone of voice, that one little bit has stuck with me and helped me the most.

It seems that one of the more common ways to communicate high energy is to bring your tone up a few octaves. Not that there is anything wrong with a low voice, but bringing it up during this phase will show that you have a high energy level and are ready to go.

A good place to bring your tone up is right off the bat with your first couple of words. Having that excitement within the first few words will really grab the prospect's attention and will bring them directly in on you.

- "**Good morning**, sir/ma'am! My name is Jason…"

Enthusiasm

Enthusiasm is tied in with excitement, but it leans heavily on the verbal element of the introduction in terms of your actual words and your verbiage. We will go more into this in the remaining two sections but, essentially, you want to clearly communicate to the prospect in a manner that represents that you are thrilled to be talking to them.

For example, rather than saying "Hey" when a prospect walks through the door or picks up the phone, a confident "Good morning sir/ma'am!" is much more enthusiastic. It's also more respectful as well. The last thing you want to do is make the customer feel disrespected. Even something as benign as saying "hey" when someone walks in the door or answers the phone may leave a sour taste in someone's mouth. That's why you should always go with the "sir/ma'am" line. By respecting the customer, you'll make them feel important and special. Worst case scenario – they'll laugh and tell you to call them by their name instead…which is actually one of the best things that could happen.

Don't leave out an E

This brings us to the last point about the three E's – use them <u>all</u> for success. If you are able to stand up straight, look someone in the eye, smile, and confidently state "Good morning, sir/ma'am!" with an upbeat tone, you will have successfully captured their full attention. You won't have this attention for very long…perhaps a few seconds at most. That's why your next few sentences need to be some of the strongest in your pitch. Whatever you say next will ultimately determine if the prospect continues to give you attention or not.

Clearly introduce yourself

You have the attention of the prospect. After your energetic welcome, the next step is to tell them who you are and what you are doing.

At this point you are not only introducing yourself as an individual, but also introducing the company that you represent as well. In a sense, the company has placed a rather large responsibility on you – you are acting as the brand ambassador, so you have to be sure you properly introduce who you work for as well. You will always want to do this because including your company in your introduction immediately adds value to you personally. If you are representing a respected brand, adding that company name will build instant credibility with the prospect.

The best way to do this is to clearly state your name, immediately followed by the company that you represent. Depending on what the situation is, you can usually go one of three ways without ever any deviation.

Let's return to our new job at the Safe Security Company. If you are calling someone on the phone, you can say **"Good morning, sir/ma'am! My name is ____ and I am reaching out to you today from Safe Security Company!"** If you are knocking on doors, you can say **"Good morning, sir/ma'am! My name is ____ and I am representing the Safe Security Company!"** Finally, if you are at the store and someone walks in, you can say **"Good morning, sir/ma'am! My name is ____ and welcome to the Safe Security Company!"**

Don't be shy about it either. You want to confidently stand behind your company name. If you are looking for ways you can avoid stating what company you represent, then there is a bigger issue at hand. We won't dive too deep into that in this book, but let's just say that it's important to believe in your company and your product.

Stating your company name shows confidence in the brand. It's important to have a unified front, where the employees and the brand all showcase confidence in each other. This means that the prospect will have an easier time trusting you AND the brand, which is crucial to close a sale. It's also important in building your credibility. Standing behind a reputable and large company is a way for you to instantly become credible in the eyes of your prospect, so definitely take advantage of that element.

We went over this before, but it's so important that we'll bring it up again. Don't forget the body language component here, too. A smile goes a long way when introducing yourself. Even if you are on the phone, people will notice when you are smiling because they can sense it in your voice.

Establish command of the conversation

After you've introduced yourself and your company you have to establish that you are in control of the call. This step is absolutely crucial because after you introduce yourself prospects will try to interject right here and steer the conversation in whatever direction they want.

If you fail to establish command right here, it gives the prospect a chance to run away from you or hang up before you even present anything.

You: "Good morning, sir/ma'am! My name is ____ and I am reaching out to you today from Safe Security Company!..."
Prospect: "Hello, thank you for calling, but I am not interested."

After something like that happens, it's almost impossible to regain control of the conversation and the attention of the prospect. You might as well just move on to the next person. As we all know, sales is a huge numbers game. The more opportunities you have to present your product or service, the more sales you will make. It's not rocket science – just basic statistics. A missed opportunity right away is a missed potential closed sale, which should be devastating for any commission-based salesperson. That's why it's crucial to take command of the call right away.

<u>State your purpose</u>

Right away, you have to have a power statement ready to go that explains the purpose of you talking or being there. The power statement should be short and concise because you want the prospect to want more from you. This is the part where you have to convince the prospect that they should listen to you. If this were a transaction, this power statement is your money, and the product that you are buying is more time with the prospect.

This power statement should be a compelling reason that they should give you more time. A good way to begin the statement is:

- "The reason for my call today is..."

Or, if you are in a face-to-face setting:

- "The reason why I am here is…"

This all might sound pretty obvious to you. If it does, then great! But you would be surprised how many sales representatives start the sales process without giving a clear and concise reason for the call without even realizing it.

Think about the last time you received a disengaging sales call from someone. More often than not, the representative probably tried to make small talk with you right away. While making small talk is good for rapport building, you want to engage the customer first to keep them active in the conversation. Small talk in the beginning will only leave people skeptical of why you are calling and who you are. Not to mention, rapport building is an entirely different stop on your road map.

Having a prospect that is skeptical of you is never a good thing. Unfortunately, we live in a world that has a growing number of scam artists and criminals in it. Now more than ever, people are highly resistant to do business with strangers. That's why it's important to establish the reason for your call right away. You don't want the prospect's head wandering away and thinking that you might not be legit.

Again with the examples of the Safe Security Company, here are some ways to state your purpose.

- "Good morning, sir/ma'am! My name is ____ and I am reaching out to you today from Safe Security Company! The reason for my call is that there have been a string of break-ins in your neighborhood. I would like to discuss your security needs with you."

- "Good morning, sir/ma'am! My name is ____ and I represent the Safe Security Company! The reason for me visiting you today is that there have been reports of a string of break-ins in your neighborhood. Now is a good time to evaluate your security needs."
- "Good morning, sir/ma'am! My name is ____ and welcome to the Safe Security Company! Due to a recent spike in local break-ins, we are running some specials on our packages. Now is a good time to evaluate your security needs.

The compelling reason of why the prospect should listen to you is that there have been a string of break-ins in the neighborhood. Ideally, no person would say "Oh, that's OK; I'm alright if someone robs me. Not interested."

It's extremely important to note that you should <u>never</u> lie for your compelling reason to listen to you. A sales position is not about lying or manufacturing problems for prospects. While some may try this, a prospect will sense it from a mile away. Not to mention, it destroys all credibility that you have, ruins your reputation, and is unethical.

This is where your knowledge of the product, the competition, the industry, and the prospect that you discovered during your C.A.L.L. preparation all come in handy. The compelling reason should be able to be both factual and pressing enough where the prospect should say "Yea, alright, I'll listen."

<u>*Have a strong handshake*</u>

If you are in a face-to-face setting, another subtle way to establish command is to be the first one to extend your hand for a handshake. By initiating the handshake, you are essentially connecting yourself to the prospect and nonverbally communicating that you will be the one to help them out.

It's important to have a strong handshake too. You don't want to be so strong that you break someone's hand, but you want it to be strong enough to show that you are a professional and you take yourself seriously. A weak handshake might destroy your credibility, so it's important to make sure yours is firm. Don't forget to look the prospect in the eyes as well!

Misconception: always ask if this is a good time

One of the biggest misconceptions that sales representatives have is that they have to ask the prospect permission to speak with them.

Phone representatives will ask "Is now a good time to call you?" while face-to-face representatives might simply state "I hope I didn't get you at a bad time!"

This was a line that I held dear for far too long. In my head, I wanted to be respectful of the prospect's time and acknowledge that if they are busy, I can reach back out to them at a better time. In fact, I believed in my rationale so much that I actually wrote a few articles in defense of it.

However, once I examined my calls from a 10,000 feet view, I began to see a trend. Wherever I gave prospects a chance to get away from me, they would often seize the opportunity and I would never be able to reach them again. The fact of the matter is this: if a prospect answers the phone or answers the door, it's a good time to talk to them. If they were in the middle of something crucial, they would either let your call go to voicemail, or just not answer the door. Rest easy - if something was on fire, the prospect would not have greeted you.

If you insist on being respectful of the prospect's time:

- "Good morning, sir/ma'am! My name is ____ and I am reaching out to you today from Safe Security Company! The reason for my call is that there have been a string of break-ins in your neighborhood. I would like to discuss your security needs with you. **I know that you are busy, so this will not take that long.**"

If you decide to say this, you are being respectful of their time, but also, not giving them a chance to wiggle away from you. Be careful though – you don't want to pigeonhole yourself to a set time. If you say that this will take no longer than five minutes, the prospect might become angry if it takes longer than that.

Final check

So, at this point, we have visited our first stop. Assuming that the prospect answered, we have properly introduced ourselves using the 3 E's (energy, excitement, and enthusiasm). We have gained the attention of the prospect, clearly introduced ourselves and our company, and have seized command of the conversation. Just for good measure too, we have respected the prospect's time. They are engaged in the conversation and ready to listen to us. Let's head on to our next stop!

Road Block: Nobody is at the First Stop

"Winning isn't everything, but wanting to win is." -Vince Lombardi, legendary football coach and NFL executive

---

We just spent a good deal of time describing what to do at the *Introduce Yourself* stop. This assumes that somebody is actually there to greet us. In a perfect world, people will always answer the door and when we call them, they will always pick up.

Unfortunately, we do not live in a perfect world. More often than not, when we arrive at our first stop nobody will be there to talk to. Either they are simply not home, or they just refuse to answer the door or pick up the phone.

If this is the case, our road trip unfortunately has come to an end, at least for now. At this point, you can do one of two things. You can either give up and go home, or try to initiate the sales process for a future opportunity. Do not give up – try to leave a convincing and powerful message. We have the potential to revisit this stop whenever someone is ready to see us.

The worst thing that we can do is give up entirely. Once we give up, the future opportunity to make the sale is gone. While this is indeed a road block, it's a minor one that can be overcame if navigated correctly.

Notes/Business cards

If you are knocking on doors, you might come across an instance where either nobody is home, or they just refuse to answer the door. If this is the case, there is unfortunately not a whole lot you can do other than revisit at a later time. If you revisit and again there is no answer, consider leaving a little note or a business card with your introduction power statements on it and a clear call to action for the prospect to contact you.

- "Hello, sir/ma'am! My name is ____ and I am reaching out to you today from Safe Security Company! The reason for me visiting here today is that there have been a string of break-ins in your neighborhood. I would like to discuss your security needs with you. Please give me a call at (555) 456-7890 at your earliest convenience."

You can either leave this note in the crevice of the front door or in the mailbox, whichever you prefer. If you are going to leave a note, don't leave a note on a ripped up scrap piece of notebook paper. This note should be just like your introduction - it should be professional. If you leave a note that looks like it was thrown together at the last minute, people might think it's a scam and will refuse to call you. Use a proper piece of paper with your company letterhead if available.

Voicemails

If you are calling somebody, you have the luxury of leaving a voicemail. This is one of the most underutilized tools in phone sales. You will notice that many representatives will simply hang up when it turns over to the voicemail recording because they want to catch the prospect in a live conversation. They believe that giving the prospect control of when they call will give them all the power in the conversation right off the bat.

While there might be a little bit of truth to this, I will make the argument that leaving a voicemail is much better than not leaving one for several reasons:

People are more paranoid now than ever before

We live in a pretty frightening time. It seems that no matter where we turn to we always see stories of scam artists and identity thieves. With the introduction of smartphones, it seems that every single person is required to enter a phone number in somewhere when registering anywhere online. Who knows where this information will end up? If I get a call from an unrecognizable number who that not leave a voicemail, I am going to assume that it's worse than a sales person – it's someone who has genuine malicious intent. You definitely don't want this to happen to you. Be a friendly voice on the voicemail assuring that you are a real person with a real company.

Leaving a voicemail gives you a better shot at a callback

By leaving encouraging and friendly voicemails you have a much better chance at having a callback than if you simply hang up. Rarely do people call back an unrecognizable number without a real voice attached to it.

If your voicemail message is clear, concise, and has real value built in for the prospect, the prospect will call back at a time that works for them. It's important to include a call-to-action, meaning that we want to clearly communicate to the prospect that they should call us back. We will go over some examples of voicemail scripting later on to help encourage callbacks.

Even if they don't call back, they have a better chance of picking up next time

Imagine this scenario. You are out to dinner with your significant other and receive a call from a random number. Of course, you are not going to answer it. The voicemail states that they are calling from a local charity and would like to speak to you about their cause and would like a call back. You think "That's a good idea.", but you're human, so you forget about it (we'll just blame the wine at dinner). A couple days later, you get another call but recognize the number as that nice charity who left a voicemail, so you pick up this time. This scenario isn't some rare phenomenon; it happens a lot more than you think.

My wife and I were going through the home-buying process. I had missed a call from a mortgage banker because I was at work and did not recognize the phone number. They left a voicemail stating who they were, what company they represented, and what they wanted to speak with me about. Because I was at work, I put it to the back burner and forgot about it. When they called back a few days later, I recognized the number, felt bad for not calling back and answered right away,

If you don't leave a voicemail, people will look your number up on search engines

Have you ever looked up your own work number? If you have not, go ahead and try it now. What you see may surprise you. You might find that nothing comes up, which is the best-case scenario. However, even if you are a real, genuine caller who works for a good, reputable company you might find a few websites with pages of complaints from disgruntled people.

If you refuse to leave a voicemail, you are basically telling people to go ahead and do their own research based off of your number without hearing your voice first. Like we said before, if you form judgmental opinions of prospects ahead of time, it might ruin your chances for a sale. The same logic applies for the prospect that forms judgmental opinions of the caller before they even speak. Don't let that happen.

This will essentially take the place of your introduction on the phone

When leaving a voicemail, this will be your introduction. It needs to be rock solid and perfect. If you just hang up, that's similar to meeting someone face to face and instantly walking away from them. What are the odds that they will be friendly to you next time you want to talk to them? In this part, we will go over some voicemail scripting to ensure that you have the highest probability of a callback.

A great voicemail for our security company situation would be:

- "Hello, sir/ma'am! My name is ____ and I am reaching out to you today from the Safe Security Company! The reason for me calling today is that there have been a string of break-ins in your neighborhood. I would like to discuss your security needs with you. Please give me a call at (555) 456-

7890 at your earliest convenience. Thank you, and I look forward to speaking with you!"

Here we left a voicemail that introduces us, introduced the company that we represent, we included a power statement, and presented clear instructions for the prospect to call us back. Remember, utilize the 3 E's (Energy, Excitement, and Enthusiasm) in your voicemail as well!

Text messaging

This is a newer way of selling that salespeople are still trying to master. Less than twenty years ago, cell phones were really only used to make calls. People disliked texting because it was cumbersome (who remembers T9 texting?) and oftentimes, people were limited on a monthly basis as to how many texts they could send and receive. I vividly remember having a brick-style cell phone that could only send/receive 200 texts in a month. I certainly would not have wanted to waste one of those texts interacting with a salesperson.

Nowadays, we all have smartphones with basically a full keyboard that appears on the screen when you are ready to text. Many cell plans have included unlimited texting as well. Because of this (and the introduction of emojis), people would rather text than have a real conversation.

Call me old-fashioned, but I subscribe to the notion that simple texting could never take the place of having a real conversation. You miss out on crucial elements such as voice inflection, rapport building, etc. Plus, it can be really easy for prospects to simply ignore or delete text messages if they don't feel like responding. They essentially have all the power in the conversation.

This is why I use texts purely as a 'call me back' tool. Of course, all this could easily change as technology and the users evolve with time. When that time comes we will have to adapt, but for now, it seems that a real conversation is more powerful for sales.

Texts are different than notes, voicemails, or emails. They are different because users dislike reading a 'wall of text,' meaning that the longer the text message, the less likely someone will finish reading the entire thing. A text should be short, simple, engaging, and to the point.

- "Hello, sir/ma'am! My name is ____ and I am texting you from the Safe Security Company! There have been break-ins in your area. I would like to discuss your security needs with you. Please give me a call at (555) 456-7890 at your earliest convenience."

Again, it includes all the elements in the basic introduction with the call to action for the prospect to get in touch with you.

Every so often, people will ask me about the use of emoticons (otherwise known as emojis). For those who do not know, an emoji is a graphic that is found on the smartphone keyboard, usually consisting of faces and relevant items. In this case, a relevant emoji would possibly be a little padlock.

The argument for the use of emojis is that it can enhance your text message and make it *pop* more for the reader. If your prospect is of the younger generation the use of emojis can go a long way with them.

Be careful, though, when using emojis – there is a significant generational and professional gap between those who use them and those who do not. The use of emojis are becoming more and more popular now with people from all generations and backgrounds, but they really have not yet made their way to the professional environment. I would stay away from emojis. Be cognizant of your audience and your professional image.

The same rule applies for text-talk, such as LOL, BRB, LMAO, etc. You are a professional representative of your brand. The prospect has to see that you are a legitimate professional; otherwise they will have a lot of trouble trusting you. If you would not say it (or in this case, spell it) during a real conversation, just avoid it.

Emails

The email is another tool that you can use to try to reach a prospect. This tool is often used as a last resort amongst professionals. Despite the fact that more and more people are going online to take care of business, it's really easy to either ignore or instantly delete an email before even reading it, especially if it comes from an unrecognized email address.

Also, with hyper advanced spam-fighting and organizational tools, you never know if your email will even reach the prospect. You might find that your email was either sent to the spam folder or sent to the "promotions and offers" folder (which nobody really ever reads).

That being said – if you have exhausted all other options to try and reach the prospect, this is a great way to throw the life preserver out there and hopefully save the opportunity. Again, be respectful, include the power statements, and include the call to action for the prospect to reach you.

- "Hello, sir/ma'am! My name is ____ and I am attempting to reach out to you from Safe Security Company! The reason for me emailing you is that I have been trying to get in contact with you to discuss the fact that there have been a string of break-ins in your neighborhood. Now is a great time to evaluate your security needs. Please give me a call at (555) 456-7890 at your earliest convenience!"

End of the road block: a live contact

The idea here is that eventually, the prospect will either answer the door next time or will give you a call. Once you make live contact, your introduction changes a little bit simply because you already stated your purpose and your compelling reason in the messages. However, your introduction should not make a radical change. It's important to remind the prospect of why they called us back in the first place.

- "Good morning, sir/ma'am! Thank you so much for calling me back. So, again, my name is ____ and I am with the Safe Security Company! I was reaching out to you because there have been reports of a string of break-ins in your neighborhood. We need to take this time to go over your security needs."

Notice how the verbiage changed a little bit. We thanked the prospect for calling us and reminded them of the compelling reason. Also, notice how we did not ask if this was a good time or say that this will only take a moment. If the prospect calls you back, it's definitely a good time for them so just press on!

Final check

If you ever encounter this road block, try your best to initiate the sales process. If you are able to successfully communicate your message to the prospect, there is likelihood that you will have the chance to pitch the prospect still at a future date. While this is not ideal, it's better than giving up. Tools such as business cards, voicemails, texts, and emails can all be used to start a conversation with the prospect. Once you attempt this, you should be persistent and keep following up with the prospect. Once you reach the prospect, you can resume your road trip and head on to stop 2!

Stop 2: Rapport Building

"No friendship is an accident." – O. Henry, 19th century American short story author

---

You've made your introduction. You have the attention of the prospect and they are fully engaged. The next stop that you'll be visiting is the *Rapport Building* stop.

Building rapport is basically the act of making a connection with the prospect. You'll commonly hear that one of the most fundamentally important elements of the sales presentation is to simply make a friend with the prospect. This is important because, as stated already, people buy from those that they like. This step is all about making that prospect a friend.

In this stop you have you make yourself as likeable as possible. If you come across as someone who the prospect does not like, your chances of closing a deal are slim. This is why rapport building is such a crucial step.

However, just like in a real road trip, it's incredibly easy to get stuck in this part because it's sometimes the most fun part. You can easily fall in the trap of small with a prospect for twenty or more minutes. While you may think that this is good for making a friend, it can actually be destructive to your sales process. Remember, you have limited time to speak to the prospect. If you spend fifteen minutes talking about your favorite sports team, you run the risk of the prospect cutting your meeting short because they have something else to attend to. That's why this step needs to be carefully plotted out before you even arrive - you can easily lose the momentum that was built up in your powerful introduction.

There are a many different ways to build rapport with a prospect, but the few that are the most effective are light conversations, gift giving, and psychological mirroring.

Light conversations

A light conversation, otherwise known as *small talk*, is one of the most recognizable ways that you can build rapport. In fact, I'll bet that when you first read the title "Rapport Building," the first thought that popped in your head was how to effectively make small talk with the prospect.

If so, then you are on the right track. A light conversation can do many things. It can put the prospect at ease, establish commonality, and you can actually learn what's important to the prospect as an individual. All of these things are important when making a friend, which is the ultimate goal of this step.

The trick is that you want to make impactful small talk with the prospect, meaning that you want to talk about things that are both relevant and important to them. If your prospect hates football, you don't want to spend five minutes talking about how amazing you think the Falcons are going to be next year. Nobody is a mind reader, so how do we figure out what's important to the prospect on an individual level?

Ask questions

The best way to discover what's important to a prospect is by asking lighthearted questions. You don't want this to be an interrogation so the questions should be conversational by nature. Ideally, you should be looking to uncover an interest or a viewpoint that you have in common.

It's important to stay away from controversial topics that could either spark a debate or inflame the prospect. Typically, I stay far away from religion, politics, and any negative current events going on. The worst thing that can happen is that you get involved with a heated debate over what the President is doing. Even if the prospect does bring them up, it's best to simply deflect the issue and take back control of the conversation. The only situation in which you should bring these topics up is if you and the prospect opinions are 100% in line with each other, which really is never the case.

Asking questions on relatively benign topics can be great for discovering a lot about the prospect. If the prospect lives in a big city, you can ask if they are happy with the result of the local sports team game last night. If they live near a group of golf courses, you can make a comment on how beautiful the courses are and ask if they ever play them. Even though it's cliché, you can even comment on the weather.

There are an infinite number of possibilities for you to open up a conversation. Here are just a couple examples of different ways to start a conversation, establish commonality and build a friendly rapport.

- "I see that you live up north in Michigan. I'm originally from there. Are you familiar with the town of Niles?"

- "Are you a big fan of baseball? Big game tonight!"

The best part about questions like these is that you can have a response ready no matter what the prospect responds with, either positive or negative.

> *You:* "I see that you live up north in Michigan. I'm originally from there. Are you familiar with the town of Niles?"
> *Prospect:* "No, never really heard of it."
> *You:* "Not surprised. It's a pretty small town. If you blink, you'll miss it. I'm sure you're ready for winter to be over here soon though! Those Michigan winters are brutal."

Even though the prospect said that they were not familiar with the town that I was from, we can still establish commonality by sympathizing with the fact that winters are harsh up north.

> *You:* "Are you a big fan of baseball? Big game tonight!"
> *Prospect:* "Not really. I'm more of a football fan."
> *You:* "Funny thing is that I couldn't help but notice that they are moving the baseball stadium from the south end of the city to the north end, and I really have not met many baseball fans up here at all!"

Again, even though the prospect said that they dislike baseball, you can still build rapport by discussing the fact that the stadium is moving towards their side of the city. This should open up a conversation about topics such as the rapid growth of the city and the football team.

It's worth noting here that you should not ask a question that you have little to no knowledge about. This step is all about establishing commonality with the prospect. If you start to ask the prospect about baseball but you have absolutely no knowledge of it, you are only hurting your chances of making a friend. It's best to be honest and only stick with topics that you either have an interest in, or at least have knowledge about.

Mix in humor

It's always a good idea to interject a certain level of lighthearted humor in the mix as well. It helps the prospect lower their defenses and makes them more open to share with you. If you are able to get the prospect to laugh (or at least smile), you're on the right path.

> *You:* "I see that you live up north in Michigan. I'm originally from there. Are you familiar with the town of Niles?"
> *Prospect:* "No, never really heard of it."
> *You:* "Not surprised. It's a pretty small town. If you blink, you'll miss it. I'm sure you're ready for winter to be over here soon though! Those Michigan winters are brutal. Nothing was worse than shoveling the driveway and 1 hour later, having another foot of snow to shovel off!"

Or, using the other example:

> *You:* "Are you a big fan of baseball? Big game tonight!"
> *Prospect:* "Not really. I'm more of a football fan."
> *You:* "I couldn't help but notice that they are moving the baseball stadium from the south end of the city to the north end and I really have not met many baseball

fans up here at all! I am sure that you are thrilled to have more traffic in your backyard!"

Again, these are simply two questions out of the thousands that you can ask. The important takeaway here is that the questions should be conversational by nature to help lower the defenses of the prospect. As mentioned before, the goal is to establish common ground with the prospect. Mixing in some humor only adds to that commonality. Friends make other friends laugh - use this to your advantage.

Be a good listener

You can ask questions until you are blue in the face but it doesn't really matter unless you are actually listening to what the prospect is saying. Make sure you are actively listening to their responses and responding appropriately.

You might be thinking that this is totally common sense and should not be part of a book on how to sell professionally. However, think about the last sales-related interaction you had where you felt like you were not being heard. Better yet, think of the last general conversation where you felt like the other person heard you, but simply did not care. I'd imagine that it has happened to you before and I bet it felt terrible. There is a huge difference between hearing and listening.

People tend to think that selling is all about fast-talking and wordplay, so a lot of salespeople seem to primarily work on those skills. However, having the ability to be a great listener is absolutely as important of a skill. By being a good listener, a prospect will feel like they are being heard, understood, and appreciated.

Being a great listener is important during this stage, but it's crucial in later steps. Here's the thing: if the prospect feels comfortable enough to open up to you during this step, you will have no problem uncovering some real, valuable information later on. You have to communicate to the prospect that you are a great listener right now at this step to get them to that comfort level.

Being a good listener involves more than just hearing the words coming out of the prospect's mouth. There are some ways you can actively listen and easily internalize what the prospect is saying while making the prospect feel at ease with you.

Here are five simple rules to remember when listening to somebody.

Smile, make eye contact and use welcoming body language

If you are in front of the prospect, a hefty responsibility is placed on you. Much of our actual communicating is done non-verbally, which means that your body language has to be welcoming and friendly. If you smile, look someone in the eye, and lean in when they are talking to you, you'll show the prospect that you are really listening and actually care.

The opposite would be to look around the room, lean back, and cross your arms. This communicates that you are either nervous or in defense mode. None of those behaviors are conducive to making a friend or active listening. The prospect will surely sense this and might withhold some valuable information from you - not to spite you, but because they might not feel like you are even listening.

Empathize

When a prospect is sharing something with you, always empathize with what they are telling you. By empathize, I don't mean to say the cliché phrase of "Oh, yes, I know *exactly* what you mean!" In any instance, you do not know what the prospect means because you have different experiences than they do. The idea here is to communicate that we are open to their point of view and would like to hear more about it.

A great way to empathize would be to say something to the effect of "I can see where you are coming from, but let me make sure I understand…"

Telling the prospect that you might understand but wanting clarification will show them that you are actually listening and have a desire understand clearly. This is important to remember not only during this phase, but during the later steps where we will be asking the prospect about their needs and problems.

Don't make it about you

One of the most annoying things that a person can do is take one of your stories and make it all about them. It's human to do so – by nature, we *love* talking about ourselves. It's everyone's favorite topic! Prospects are not immune to this rule. When they are talking about themselves and their experiences, don't instantly make it about you. They don't want to hear about you – they want to talk about themselves!

If you keep the conversation focused on the prospect and not you, they will keep opening up to you and will share more and more with you. They will feel as if they are being appreciated as an individual.

Additionally, don't attempt to "one-up" the prospect with a story of your own. Not only will you come across as a bragger, but it will become clear to the prospect that you were only interested in talking about your own experiences, rather than listening to them.

Don't interject or interrupt

When a prospect is talking, sometimes it's easy to want to interrupt them. If they start to say something that you have a response for, it's almost second nature to interject and respond to what they said right away. If a prospect is talking, it's important to let them finish their entire train of thought. Interrupting will only make them mad and will once again show them that you care more about what you have to say than listening to them.

This is important to remember during the later step of objection handling. We will go over this in further detail, but even if a prospect is telling you something that is 100% incorrect, interrupting them will only plant the seeds for an argument, which is the last thing you want to happen.

Everything is important to the prospect

The most important thing to remember is that no matter the topic, if the prospect is talking about it to you, it's important to them. It doesn't really matter how silly or insignificant it might seem to you. If the prospect is comfortable enough to share it with you, it's important to them and should be treated as such.

If you brush things off with phrases like "Oh, that's really neat, but let's move on…" the prospect might feel embarrassed or unappreciated. This is something that you definitely do not want to happen. Whatever the prospect is telling you, make sure you communicate that you are excited about the material and are interested in the story.

As mentioned before, all of this stuff might seem like common sense, but it's important to remember during the course of our road trip, especially when we actually get to some of the more intensive question & answer stops, such as the *Discovering a Need* stop and the *Objection Handling* stop.

If you are able to show the prospect that you are actually listening to them and make them feel as if they are being heard and appreciated, you'd be amazed at what they will tell you later on when you ask a question that is more intrusive and thought-provoking. This step is where you lay the foundation for that.

Take mental notes

It's important to note here that whatever you learn during this step should be remembered for next time you meet the prospect. Of course, if you are in a face-to-face setting, taking notes in the middle of a conversation might seem weird and off-putting to the prospect, so you have to remember what the prospect said and take notes as soon as you are done with the conversation and away from the prospect. If you are on the phone, you have the luxury of taking notes in real time.

This is why so many companies have Customer Relationship Management (CRM) software. If you have this software provided to you, take full advantage of it. As soon as you are done with the sales call, record everything you remember about what the prospect said. If you do not have CRM software available to you a simple computer spreadsheet, a paper notebook, or even a rolodex will work very well. All you need is an organized way to record and recall information that works for you.

The notes don't have to be very detailed, but should jog your memory of the conversation.

1. Mr. Smith
    i. Not a fan of baseball. Likes football. His team is the Falcons.
    ii. Discussed quarterback and how great he plays.

If you do this, you won't have to ask those same rapport discovery questions over and over again. You can simply come back and say:

- "I know that you said you liked football better than baseball – you must be really excited about the quarterback this year. He has been on fire in the preseason."

If you fail to take proper notes and come back next time asking about baseball, you'll lose a certain level of credibility. The prospect might assume that you were not listening to them last time, which puts you in a very awkward place. Remember, you might call on hundreds of people every month, but you might be but a handful of salespeople who calls on him. The conversations you have might stick out more in his memory than yours, so definitely be sure to take the proper notes afterwards.

Some presentations last for minutes, while others can last hours. You might be thinking that it'll be nearly impossible to remember what happened during these early steps. In the section before this, we went over the basic rules of proper listening. If you remember to do all of those, you will have no problem recalling what happened during the presentation.

Give gifts

Think about the last time someone tried to get you to do something. Odds are, at some point during your conversation, they gave you some kind of gift. The gift could have been anything from a pen to a compliment to a discount, but I'll bet that the person gave you something for free. If that was the case, you might have felt a slight obligation to 'return the favor' and do whatever that other person wanted you do to. The act of giving a gift is one of those universal principles that are held dear amongst sales representatives everywhere. One of the reasons for this is that salespeople are seeking to take advantage of the *norm of reciprocity*.

The *norm of reciprocity* essentially is the societal expectation that people will respond positively if you do something that benefits them. On the flip side, it also means that people will respond negatively if you do something that harms them.

If we look at this from the perspective of our road trip, this can be compared to having people who are willing to help us along the way because we helped them out. For example, if we are driving along and one of our tires goes flat because we ran over a nail, we will have to stop and get it fixed somewhere. It will be much easier if we know the mechanic and have helped him/her out in the past. The *norm of reciprocity* states that the mechanic should help us quickly, efficiently, and perhaps even at a discounted rate.

In terms of sales, the act of giving a prospect a free gift that benefits them should compel them to act favorably, such as disclosing some valuable information or being receptive to hearing our pitch. You have probably seen this in action before without even realizing it. One example that you might have come across is during career fairs. You will often see dozens of company booths lined up in a row, all staffed with well-trained and capable recruiters. You will also notice that each booth has a series of free gifts for you to take, such as pens, notebooks, USB sticks, etc. Ideally, you should feel obligated to consider working for the company because they provided you with a free gift.

This brings us to our second reason that salespeople are always giving out gifts: a gift is a subtle and inexpensive way to advertise your company. If you walk up to a job fair booth and receive a mousepad from McDonald's, you might be compelled to eat there more simply from looking at it every time you use the computer. You might also be compelled to call the HR rep again to check your application status.

When you are giving out gifts, you should look to accomplish the same two things: taking advantage of the norm of reciprocity and subtly advertising your brand.

The Mint Example

If you are attempting to close a sale right there in the moment, the norm of reciprocity can be a powerful tool for you. This is not conjecture or wishful thinking – it's actually backed by science.

In 2002, researchers David Strohmetz, Bruce Rind, Reed Fisher, and Michael Lynn published an article in the Journal of Applied Social Psychology [3] that essentially shows the act of giving gifts can translate to real increases in revenue.

The study focused on waiters and waitresses (referred to as the wait staff) and how the simple act of giving customers mints with the bill increases the tips for the wait staff. The results are pretty amazing to say the least:

The control group consisted of the wait staff giving the customers no mints with the bill. It's important to note that the level of service did not change from the control group at all.

The first group consisted of the wait staff giving the customers mints along with the bill, without mentioning the mints at all. **This increased tips by around 3% against the control group**.

The second group consisted of the wait staff bringing mints by hand and asking the table if anybody would care for mints before he/she left. **This increased tips by 14% against the control group.**

The third and final group consisted of the wait staff bringing mints along with the check. As he/she was walking away from the table, they would turn around and say something like "Oh, because you all were so good and fun to wait on, here are some more mints for you." **This increased tips by an astonishing 21% against the control group.**

The final conclusion of the study was that the norm of reciprocity was responsible for increased tips, not mood management or impression management. They also concluded that the third group took advantage of personalization, meaning that they made the gift exclusive for the customers because they were "good customers and fun to serve." The personalization of the gift was responsible for the dramatic increase in tips.

This shows that the act of giving personalized gifts can translate to real, tangible, quantifiable increases in revenue for the individual or the company. So, how can you as a sales representative take advantage of this principle by adding it to the *Rapport Building* stop?

Give physical gifts

Physical gifts, such as company pens, mouse pads, coffee cups, and clothing, are great ways that you can appropriately gift the prospect. If you work for a company who offers these gifts to you to give out, take full advantage of it. It helps with reciprocity, and as stated before, will serve as a subtle advertisement for repeat business.

If we take the study to heart, making the gift personalized and giving a little bit extra can literally mean the difference between making a closed sale or not. Remember, this step is all about making the prospect like and trust you.

Let's continue with the two examples from before to show how this can be done properly.

- "I have this letter opener to hand out, but since we are both from Michigan, here is an extra one for you."

- "I have a beverage koozie for you here, but since we are both Falcons fans, here is a couple extra to keep your drinks nice and cold while we watch them win this season."

In both instances we took the basic gift, made it personal for the prospect, established more commonality, and gave something a little extra. According to social psychology, the prospect should feel a sense of obligation to treat you like a friend and perhaps even be more receptive to making a purchase from you.

At the very minimum, they should at least feel obligated to hear your pitch. Remember, at any point during our road trip, the prospect can suddenly decide that it's over and end it. We have to make sure that we earn more and more time with the prospect. This step and the act of gift giving are all about earning that time.

Give a recommendation

The act of giving gifts does not start and end with a physical product. You can also offer a recommendation to the prospect as your pitch. The can be anything from a local secret to actually doing something above and beyond for the prospect right there.

If you are on the phone and not able to give a tangible gift to someone, try this out.

Here is an example of a recommendation:

- "I have a little secret – being that we are both from Michigan, I'll share it with you. If you ever find yourself by the Upper Peninsula, check out Tahquamenon Falls State Park. They have probably the best waterfall that you can find in Michigan. Great spot for a family picture or a hike."

We did not say anything really special or extraordinary, but the simple recommendation and the fact that it's important to you will show commonality with the prospect and they will feel gratitude for you sharing it with them. The principle of reciprocity will still hold true here, even without a tangible gift.

Here is another example. This time, we'll provide a service with the recommendation.

- "I have a neat spot that I love to go to and watch the Falcons games. It's located in downtown Woodstock. I'm friends with the owner there – I could definitely give him a call and have you and your friends eat and drink using my discount!"

This one goes a little above and beyond the call of duty. If you are going to go with a service on top of your recommendation, make sure you actually follow through with the service. Nothing is worse than over-promising and under-achieving. Again, the principle of reciprocity will hold true here.

This is something that you can do either on the phone or in a face-to-face setting. If your company does not offer complimentary gifts, this is a fantastic alternative.

Give compliments

Let's say that you are brand new to the area and don't have any recommendations. Or, let's say that you are on the phone with someone in Arizona and have never been there before. As we have already established, lying is a bad idea, so we never want to make something up and recommend it. In this scenario, a compliment is a great go-to gift.

Compliments are underrated. Most people hardly get complimented during their day, so it's refreshing to hear one. Think about the last time you were genuinely complimented by someone. It probably made your day much better and lifted your mood. If you can make your prospect feel like that, you've done a great job, and the reciprocity principle will hold true.

When I was a student at Purdue University, there were two students who would stand in the middle of campus every day. They would hold a sign that said "free compliments" and would proceed to compliment everybody who walked by them. Often it was something as simple as a "Hey, I really like those shoes." Soon, these students became known as the 'compliment guys' and they became a staple of university life. Their story was picked up by several big-time newspapers and eventually, they went on tour to other universities, paying compliments to students there. Looking back, students have stated that hearing the free compliments was what helped them through tough weeks and that they actually walked out of their way to hear a compliment from them. A free compliment is a fantastic way to make someone (including prospects) feel good.

When complimenting someone, make sure you make it genuine and personalized. Impersonal and false compliments will have the opposite effect.

Here are some ways we can effectively complement a prospect in a face-to-face setting:

- "I noticed that you have gorgeous landscaping. I love how green your grass is."

- "You have a beautiful home. I love the decorations!"

- "Are those family photos on your desk? You have a great looking family!"

These compliments are personal because they are pointing out something that is unique to the prospect individually. Again, the compliment must be genuine and you must not come off as you being nosy or slimy.

On the phone, it can be a little more difficult to compliment a person without knowing a whole lot about them. When you pick up on something during the light conversation, you can insert a compliment at that point.

Here is an example of how we can do that:

- "Your son goes to Michigan State? That's very impressive. You must be extremely proud!"

- "You are a nurse? My goodness – I have the most respect for nurses. You do amazing work. Thank you for all that you do."

Again, personalized compliments go a long way with prospects. It's something that will make them feel good and should trigger the principle of reciprocity.

Overall, if you are successful in giving the prospect a gift, whether it's a simple branded pen or a compliment, you will be more likeable to the prospect and it will greatly help with your rapport building. Not to mention, you will have the *norm of reciprocity* on your side, which will make the rest of your road trip much easier.

Psychological mirroring

Psychological mirroring is the final element of rapport building and is also the most subtle one. That being said, it's arguably one of the most powerful methods that salespeople use for rapport building. It's so powerful that master salespeople use this during their entire presentation too.

Psychological mirroring refers to two people acting in the same manner. Often times, it's done unintentionally between groups of people. It can be seen in families, close friends, and coworkers who have similar phrases, body language, hand gestures, and overall attitude. It can also be seen between complete strangers while they are conversing.

This is a great tool to use for rapport building. If you can mirror the prospect, they will feel as if you two are similar. Their brain will identify you as a friend, rather than a threat. This can lead to quick rapport building and to a high level of trust.

There are four main ways you can mirror someone to build rapport.

1. Body language mirroring
2. Tone and tempo mirroring
3. Verbal mirroring
4. Emotional mirroring

Body language mirroring

Mirroring a prospect's body language is a good way you can get 'in sync' with them. The tactics are somewhat self-explanatory. If the prospect is sitting up straight in the chair, you should sit up as well. If the prospect has their arms on their desk, consider placing your arms on your legs or in your lap.

It's important to note that 100% direct imitation can possibly be seen as mockery, so it's best to keep it general. For example, if the prospect kicks their feet up, you would not do the same. Rather, look to put your arm over the back of the chair to mimic the relaxed body language of the prospect.

This can be a catch-22 though. If the prospect is displaying negative body language, such as crossing their arms or looking away from you, you would obviously not want to encourage that and mirror it. Only mirror the positive behavior.

It should be noted here that mirroring body language is only an option if you are in a face-to-face format. If you are over the phone, this is ultimately impossible to do.

Tone and tempo mirroring

Mirroring a prospect's tone of voice and tempo of speech is another fantastic way to get 'in sync' with them. If the prospect likes to talk fast, it's beneficial for you to speed things up. If the prospect is talking with a high tone of voice, raise your tone up a few octaves.

This is one of the most subtle ways you can mirror the prospect. It's usually unnoticeable unless you make a drastic change in the middle of your conversation. If you are going to do this, it's something that you should pick up on right away at the beginning of the conversation and employ as soon as possible. This is a great tactic for phone sales representatives who cannot physically see the prospect. That being said, face-to-face representatives can absolutely benefit from this as well.

Verbal mirroring

Verbal mirroring refers to the phraseology that your prospect exhibits. This means that if your prospect uses informal verbiage, a good way to quickly build rapport is to use some of the same language. The same goes for if your prospect uses formal language.

For example, if your prospect uses the word "cool" a lot, use that word too. If your prospect prefers to keep things formal and uses the word "sir or ma'am" a lot when speaking to you, you had better use the same verbiage.

Here is an example of how to do this properly:

Prospect: "Yes, we enjoy hiking and discovering **cool**, unknown places that are off the beaten path."
You: "Oh, you will definitely like this place then. The waterfalls are really **cool** to see in person. Make sure you bring a camera!"

It's very important to note here that no matter what the case is, it's never acceptable to use foul language, even if your prospect is using it. Unless you personally know the prospect and are close friends with him/her, using 'bad words' is unprofessional and never a good idea for rapport building. Much like the logic behind using emojis and text-talk, you are a professional representative of the company and the brand. Using foul language is a direct violation of the professionalism that you are supposed to be displaying. Keep it clean, no matter what the prospect says to you.

Emotional mirroring

Emotional mirroring consists of empathizing with the prospect and being on 'their side' when it comes to their mental state. It does not matter if the prospect is going through a great day, or a bad day. Empathizing with the prospect and coming from a position of understanding is a great way to show them that you are not only listening, but care about how they are feeling. Both of which are very important when building rapport.

Again, here is an example of this in action:

Prospect: "To be honest, today has been really tough. I had someone quit on me today without notice and it's thrown a monkey wrench into my operation."
You: "Oh no...I am sorry to hear that. It's always incredibly frustrating when employees decide to leave without any warning. What's worse, it seems like it's getting harder and harder to find good people to begin with!"

In this case, we were able to empathize with the prospect and agree that his feelings of anger and frustration are validated. This communicates that you are both on the same page and you feel the same way about it as he does.

If you are able to successfully do the above four mirroring tactics, the prospect will feel 'in sync' with you and will feel more comfortable talking to you and be more receptive to what you are saying. They will trust you and will possible be open to making a purchase from you.

The concept of mirroring in sales is one that can be a bit controversial because it's extremely easy for a salesperson to go overboard and flat-out mimic the prospect in an obvious manner. If this happens, the prospect may become upset or embarrassed. The mirroring has to be done in an extremely subtle way as to avoid detection from the prospect. Do your best as to not become a caricature of the prospect.

Final check

We are at the end of our *Rapport Building* stop. At this stop, our goal was to gain the trust of the prospect and become as likeable as possible. This can be accomplished through the acts of making light conversation, gift giving, and psychological mirroring.

At this stage in our road trip, the prospect should like us and should be open to talk about their needs as a potential customer. People buy from those that they like so if we were able to accomplish that during this stop, we are ready to move on to the next stop!

Stop 3: Discovering a Need

"The art and science of asking questions is the source for all knowledge." - Thomas Berger, 20th century American novelist

---

The next stop on our road trip is one of the most intensive stops that we will visit. On this stop, we will be asking a series of questions that will help us either discover a problem that the prospect is currently having or discover a need that is currently being unfulfilled.

It might surprise you that a lot of sales representatives skip this step entirely. Perhaps you have experienced it before yourself when a salesperson presented a product or service to you without identifying a solid need or desire for it on your part. In that situation, you probably did not make a purchase.

A few years back, I took my car in for a standard oil change. Bear in mind that my car has a lot of miles on it. Usually a simple oil change appointment will morph into a full-blown inspection of everything under the hood. Quite often the mechanic will come over to me, explain what needs to be repaired or replaced, and why they need to do it. I'll usually authorize them to do whatever needs to be done to ensure my safety in the car. However, this one particular instance, the mechanic came over to me and simply said something along the lines of "I can replace your air filter for $29.99." I'm not a car guy, so I really had no idea what the air filter was for, but I declined the offer because he never said why I needed it. He never identified a problem that it was causing or would cause. Therefore, I did not see any value in replacing something. It will be the same story for all of your sales pitches if you don't discover or identify a problem/need for the prospect.

One of the reasons why some salespeople have such a poor reputation is because some of them invent needs for prospects, rather than discovering them. Even worse is when salespeople make-up benefits of their product or service to fulfill the need. When you fabricate a reason why the prospect needs to purchase your good, you might be able to close a sale right there, but you will have some problems after the fact:

- Once the prospect figures out they don't need your product, they will have buyer's remorse.
- They will feel like you "pulled a fast one" on them and will feel cheated.
- Your chance of a repeat buyer or a loyal customer diminishes.
- Depending on your return policy, you might either lose a sale or have an infuriated customer.

None of these are good for business and they are certainly not good for your reputation. Working in sales, your reputation is more important than you might think. If you have the reputation for being a 'slimy' salesperson, you not only hurt your own business, but hurt the brand that you represent as well.

This is why it's incredibly important that you discover a true need or a real problem that the prospect has. When you uncover a true need or a real problem that they are experiencing you will have the following benefits:

- They will feel good about what they have purchased.
- The likelihood that they will rescind on the sale will decrease.
- They have a strong chance of becoming a loyal customer to you and the brand.
- Your will develop a solid reputation for being a helpful salesperson.

If you have all of the above working for you, you'll find that prospects will be more open to hearing about your product/service, will close at higher rates, and will come back to possibly purchase more when the time is right.

The question is, how can we discover true needs or real problems from the prospect?

Ask open-ended questions

Fortunately, it's actually much easier to discover true needs than it is to invent them. The reason why it is so much easier is because if you have followed the steps before this and have a great rapport going with the prospect, they will simply tell you their needs when asked! Just like during the rapport building process, the key here is to keep the questions lighthearted and conversational.

When you are asking discovery questions, phrasing is important. It's important because you want to ask the questions in a manner that will not only engage the prospect, but will also lead you directly to uncovering a problem. This is why you cannot just ask random questions - you have to ask the correct questions that require the prospect to converse with you. By far the best way to engage your prospect is to ask **open-ended questions**.

An open-ended question is one where the prospect has to respond with a whole sentence, rather than just a simple "yes" or a "no." They require more thought and essentially require the prospect to have a real conversation with you.

Here is an example of a closed-ended question that should be avoided:

> *You:* "Well, it looks like your house is already covered with another security company - are they sufficiently covering you?"
> *Prospect:* "Yep!"

If you ask a question like that, the prospect will answer with either a "yes" or a "no." In this case, there is no way you can uncover a need because the prospect just shut you down and said that they are sufficiently covered. There is no opportunity to have a conversation about it because in their mind, they just told you that they are good to go.

You might be thinking - what if the customer tells you "no" rather than "yes" in that case? While that might be a possibility, most prospects will not open up to you right away and tell you that they are having problems. You have to dig for them.

Even is the prospect does respond with a "no," you still have to ask a follow up question to clarify what exactly is bothering them about their current provider. That follow up question will more than likely be an open-ended question anyway. Asking closed-ended questions only puts more work on you, and turns the conversation from a lighthearted talk to an interrogation of sorts.

Take this as an example: imagine that you are walking into a retail store to find a certain type of item. You are greeted by a sales associate who asks you "Can I help you find anything today?" In most cases, you will probably say something like "No, I'm just looking" even though you are there to find something specific! It's not that you are lying or being rude to the sales associate, you are just giving a pattern response to a closed-ended question. The same idea applies here: even if they are having a problem, a closed-ended question will (in most cases) result in you not being able to uncover the problem.

This idea might seem easy to understand and even easier to execute. Interestingly enough, many people struggle with this. Questions that you might think are open-ended might actually not be. Here is an example of a question that looks like an open-ended one, but is actually closed-ended.

> *You:* "Well, it looks like your house is already covered with another security company - how are they treating you?"
> *Prospect:* "Good!"

Although they did not answer with either a "yes" or a "no," they answered with a one-worded response. Again, if this happens, you will find it very difficult to backtrack and uncover a problem if they just told you that they are being treated well.

Here is another closed-ended question disguised as an open-ended question:

> *You:* "Looks like your house is covered with another company. Do you have any ways in which you'd like to see your service improve?"
> *Prospect:* "No, not really."

In general, any questions that can be answered with either "yes," "no," or a one-worded answer should be avoided. The point of discovery questions are to engage the prospect, get them talking to you, and have them present to you a real issue or a need that they have. If a prospect tells you a need or a problem that they have, they are essentially taking ownership of the need or the problem, which makes it more difficult for them to ignore when it comes to decision-making time.

Here is an example of an open-ended question that engages the prospect:

> *You:* "Looks like your house is covered with another company. What do you look for in a security company?"
> *Prospect:* "Well, I generally look for superior response time and constant monitoring."

In this example, there was no way that the prospect could have answered with a simple "yes" or "no." That question requires the prospect to put some thought into the response and provide an answer as to what is important to them individually. In this case, we discovered that superior response time and constant monitoring are important.

Here is another example of an open-ended question:

> *You:* "I see that you already have coverage with another company - what made you choose them over anyone else?"
> *Prospect:* "Well, they provide me with good coverage at a fair price."

In this case, we discovered that the prospect cares about value and is seeking to get the most bang for his/her buck.

One final example of an open-ended question:

You: "I see that you do not currently have coverage with any security company - what is holding you back?"
Prospect: "Well mostly, price. Most companies have high rates and I cannot afford to have another high monthly payment."

In this particular case, we discovered that price is a major factor for the prospect.

The main point here is that the above questions get the prospect talking. They engage the prospect, require them to think a little bit, and provide a response that will hopefully give you an opportunity to discover a need or a problem.

Don't stop until you uncover a need

Asking open-ended questions is a great way to get the prospect talking about their current situation in a conversational format. You can learn a lot simply by the answers your prospect gives you. However, more often than not, you'll run into a situation where the prospect won't divulge the information that you want from just one question.

If you ask a question and get a vague response, don't give up and go to the next step. Rather, keep on asking questions until you get your answer. The discovery step is one of the most intensive steps because unless you are able to discover a true need or a problem that the prospect is currently having, it will be very difficult to have a successful pitch.

For example, if we have the following scenario:

> *You:* "Looks like your house is covered with another company. What made you choose them over anyone else?"
>
> *Prospect:* "I'm honestly not too sure. We just picked them because that's what my parents have and they like it."

The prospect did not really tell us anything of value here. While it may appear that the prospect chose this because of their family loyalty to the brand, that doesn't always mean that there are not problems or needs that they have personally. If this is the case, we should ask clarification discovery questions.

> *You:* "I see. Well, they certainly do provide adequate coverage, so your parents have good judgement. I'm just curious though - if you had a choice, what would you personally look for in a security company?"
>
> *Prospect:* "Well, we just had our first child, so we would want something that fully protects the house, yet gives us the most bang for our buck."

Right there, we uncovered that the prospect has just had a child and that the finances are probably a little tighter than they were before. Obviously, the safety of the family is important to the prospect, but they require something that won't break the bank. This information would have never been uncovered had we simply stopped asking discovery questions after the first response.

Let's look at another example of how we can ask multiple clarification questions to uncover a need.

You: "I see that you do not currently have coverage with any security company - what has prevented you from covering yourself?"

Prospect: "Not really, sure. I don't think that my house needs it."

You: "I wish that no house needed it; in a perfect world, they wouldn't. This world isn't perfect though. Tell me about what you are currently doing now to protect your house?"

Prospect: "Well, we generally keep our doors and windows locked, plus we have a couple of guns to help too."

You: "Sounds like you are doing all the right things. What concerns me though is what happens when nobody is home. What is your plan of action if someone breaks in when you aren't there?"

Prospect: "I guess I don't really know. Look, I see that it's important, but the prices for security systems are just too high."

In this example, we had a prospect who began with the statement that they did not need coverage because they keep everything locked up and had firearms in the house for protection. Only upon asking about a plan of action in case nobody was home did the prospect reveal that price is what's holding them back from a purchase.

All that considered, this does not mean that you should ask 22 questions in a row until you discover something. That will not only make the prospect feel interrogated, but will make you feel uncomfortable. While there is no magic number of discovery questions that you should ask, generally speaking, the more questions you ask, the less the prospect will give you. If you can get what you want from a few basic questions, stop right there.

That being said, for some industries and some salespeople that work with simple and easy to understand products/services, only two or three questions might be necessary. For others who operate in a more complicated industry or with complex products, more questions might be required. The key is to be efficient enough in your discovery questioning to uncover an angle that you wish to pursue as soon as possible.

This is where the call preparation that we did ahead of time back before we left for our road trip comes into play. If you have a general, basic idea of where you want to direct the call, the discovery questions should be strategic and should lead the prospect down that path.

Converse, don't interrogate

If there is one thing you should remember from this stop, it's that you should ask these questions in a conversational format and not interrogate the prospect.

If you interrogate the prospect, they will quickly realize that you are hounding them for information and will clam up or even lie just to end the conversation. If you keep everything in the same lighthearted format as you did during the rapport building step, you should have no problem getting information.

One of the key ways to make it conversational is to empathize with the prospect, no matter what their response is. Whatever you do, don't make the prospect feel foolish for doing it their current way, no matter how illogical it may seem. A prospect who feels foolish might become embarrassed and defensive, which is something that you don't want. Here is the same example as before to illustrate this point:

Prospect: "Well, we generally keep our doors and windows locked, plus we have a couple of guns to help too."

You: "**Sounds like you are doing all the right things**. What concerns me though is what happens when nobody is home. What is your plan of action if someone breaks in when you aren't there?"

The prospect essentially stated that they do not need any security systems in place because they already have their own system in place where they keep the doors locked and have firearms. Rather than asking another question right away, we empathized with the prospect and applauded their way of thinking before presenting another question.

If we had asked question after question without empathizing at all, the dialogue would have gone something like this:

You: "I see that you do not currently have coverage with any security company - what has prevented you from covering yourself?"
Prospect: "Not really, sure. I don't think that my house needs it."
You: "Really? Tell me about what you are currently doing now to protect your house?"
Prospect: "We keep the windows and doors locked. We also have firearms."
You: "Oh. Well, that's not enough. What is your plan of action if someone breaks in when you aren't there?"
Prospect: "I don't know. Look, thanks for calling, I'm really not interested though."

Instead of a conversation, your discovery step became an argument. You were not even able to get your product pitch out before the prospect shut you down. When the conversation devolves into a point-counterpoint argument, nobody wins. This makes the prospect feel uncomfortable and interrogated, which will cause you to lose all your momentum that you have built up so far.

The only time an interrogation works is when the police are questioning a suspect. Even then, it might not work. In that scenario, the suspect is usually detained and must answer the questions or suffer some legal-related consequences. Unlike the suspect, a prospect can walk away at any time or hang up with zero repercussions to them. Keep it simple, empathize, throw some humor in there, and just remember to keep it friendly!

Ask prepared, rehearsed, and strategic questions

It's important to only ask questions that you already have an answer for. One of the worst things that could happen to a sales representative is to get blindsided with a response to which you have no rebuttal for.

We are not psychics or mind-readers, so the best way to ensure that you do not get hit with one of these is to have a planned set of 'go-to' questions that you ask every prospect, no matter the situation. These questions should be analyzed before you leave for your road trip and every answer should be planned prior to asking. You should have something prepared for each answer so whatever the prospect says, you are prepared.

Again, let's continue with the security example:

- "What do you look for in a security company?"

This is a basic, open-ended discovery question that can be asked in any industry or any sale situation. Just replace "security company" with your type of product or your service.

Now, we can break down the many different answers to this question. The prospect could respond with any of the following:

1. Price
2. Value
3. Service
4. Response time
5. Monitoring
6. Reputation
7. Convenience

There are probably more than seven possible answers; but if you ask the question you're probably going to get an answer that falls into one of those categories. This is where your research and your knowledge of your company product/service comes in handy. If you are able to name off benefits of your product from each category, you will have no problems addressing a response. Ideally, your company should provide you with sufficient training on all of these categories, but it's always helpful to do some research on your own as well.

A great way to ensure that you have all these points covered is to write a little cheat sheet for yourself to review before every sales call. Writing down what your company or product excels in is a great way to confidently ask questions that you will have an answer for. If you were working with the security system, your notes might look like this:

1. Price - Comparable to the competition
2. Value - More services are offered at the same price
3. Service - 24 hour live customer support
4. Response time - 25% faster than the competition
5. Monitoring - 24 hour monitoring
6. Reputation - Newer company, 5 star review online
7. Convenience - Internet app based, access any time

By having these jotted down you can start to formulate strategic discovery questions that lead the prospect to reveal a need or a problem that your company is well-suited to fix. As with everything else, you'll be thrown a curveball every now and again. Sometimes, someone might respond with "I don't know." You won't get the "I don't know" response very often, but when you do, you can respond with something along the lines of "Well, similar people in your situation have asked for these traits…" then go on to name some of your best qualities. If the customer answers in the affirmative, you can take that as a sign that whatever you listed are indeed important to them.

The main point here is to only ask questions in which you have already prepared an answer for. Even better, only ask questions that will direct the prospect to sharing a need that you already know is a common one that your product solves perfectly.

Let's say that our security system beats the competition in terms of services offered. We offer 24 hour monitoring and a response rate that is faster than the competition. We know this because we have done the call preparation and have done sufficient research ahead of time. When talking to this individual prospect, we want to discover if monitoring and response rate are problems for them. Here is an example of a couple clarification discovery questions to figure it out:

> *You:* "Looks like your house is covered with another company. What made you choose them over anyone else?"
> *Prospect:* "I'm honestly not too sure. We just picked them because that's what my parents have and they like it."
> *You:* "They have certainly been around for a while here and have a loyal customer base. However, a lot of people I talk to are becoming concerned as to what happens if someone breaks in when they are not home. What is your plan of action in case this happens?"
> *Prospect:* "Well, we usually arm our systems when we leave the house, so the police should be notified if that happens."
> *You:* "Great - arming your system already puts you ahead of what a lot of other folks are doing. However, it seems that more often than not, when people break in they get in and out pretty quickly. By the time the police arrive they are already gone. Tell me about your current system response rate."
> *Prospect:* "Not too sure. You know, I guess we kind of just hope that they call the police quickly so they can get there in time, but I hear it takes a while."

We accomplished everything that we wanted to right there. We asked multiple discovery questions in a lighthearted, conversational format. We knew ahead of time that we offer a superior response rate and a monitoring service that the competition does not offer, so we directed the prospect towards that direction by asking strategic open-ended questions. Eventually, the prospect said that they simply hope that the police arrive on time and really don't know the response rate.

Notice that we did not invent a problem or a need here. We uncovered the fact that the prospect has a problem when it comes to response rate and has a need for quick police action. Both of which our company can solve.

All of this was accomplished by simply asking the prospect what they are currently doing and what their plans are if something else happens. Although we have been primarily sticking with the example of a security company, you can apply the methods to any industry and any product by simply knowing your competitive advantage and having some key discovery questions selected and prepared ahead of time.

Final check

At this stop in our road trip, we have discovered the true needs and real problems our prospect is experiencing. We prepared well in advance and used the lessons we learned during our C.A.L.L. preparation to craft open-ended and strategic discovery questions that get the prospect talking. We asked these questions in a lighthearted and conversational format. We certainly did not interrogate the prospect with a barrage of closed-ended questions.

By keeping it friendly, we uncovered some great information about what the prospect needs from our company. If the prospect's problems/needs are a good fit with what our company offers, we now have a way to build value in our product and can head on to the next stop in our road trip.

Once we have this information, take a deep breath before leaving for the next stop. Enjoy the surroundings one last time. The next few stops are some of the longest and most technical stops that we will encounter.

Stop 4: The Pitch

"To be persuasive we must be believable; to be believable we must be credible; to be credible we must be truthful." - Edward R. Murrow, CBS journalist and broadcaster

---

Our next stop, known as the pitch, is the bread-and-butter of your trip. It's a little difficult to accurately describe how important this is. This stop will essentially make or break your entire road trip, so it's important to ensure it is completed perfectly. In this stop, the goal is to effectively communicate to the prospect that our product/service is perfect <u>for them</u>. By the time we are finished, the prospect should have a clear understanding of the features & benefits of your product/service and be able to relate the positive aspects to their current situation.

Many sales professionals believe that a salesperson is only as good as their pitch. I happen to agree with them. I know that so far in this book, we have said that every step is crucial to the overall goal of earning a sale. This is not taking away from that - for the pitch to work, every previous step must be done. That being said, you can have the best introduction, build a large amount of rapport, and ask all the right discovery questions, but unless you can follow up with a great pitch the entire sales call will fall apart and simply turn into a friendly conversation. It's arguably the most important step in this process.

The idea here is that we describe the product as it pertains to the prospect. We will elaborate on this later on, but the general principle is to take what we learned in the *Discovering a Need* stop and formulate a pitch around that specific problem/need. This is the time to put your product/service in the limelight. You will not only be describing all the positive features & benefits, but will also relate them specifically to your prospect. That's why often times this is the longest stop that you will make in your road trip.

Of course, there is indeed a fine line - if you rush through this stop, your prospect will not gain an adequate appreciation of what you have to offer. If you spend too much time here, they will get bored and uninterested. The pitch cannot be an hour long endeavor - it has to be long enough to get your point communicated to the prospect, but short enough as to not let the prospect get tired of hearing you talk.

Much like the previous stops, the pitch is comprised of several different components, each having a set purpose. Similar to a mathematical formula, each component of the pitch needs to be done correctly, otherwise it will fall apart and you will not see a desirable result. The components of the pitch are:

1. The transition
2. The why
3. The features, advantages, & benefits
4. The proof
5. The price

The transition

The transition step is basically your statement that signals the prospect that you are now going from conversation-mode to business-mode. Usually, this will only be a single sentence. The idea behind this transition statement is to officially enter the 'hardball' part of your sales call, where you will not only be pitching your product, but handling objections and closing the prospect. In a sense, the transition statement is almost the point of no return. Once you transition to this point of the call, you should not be going back to the *Rapport Building* stop, or the *Discovering a Need* stop. Once you transition there is no going back, so make sure that you have everything you need before transitioning.

Think of the transition statement in terms of driving a manual car. Personally, I do not have a lot of experience with manual transmission cars. I have only owned automatic transmission vehicles, so I really never bothered to learn how to drive a stick shift. Last time I went home to Michigan for Christmas, my brother-in-law was showing us his Jeep that he essentially rebuilt and fixed up from scratch. He asked me if I wanted to go for a ride to check it out. I was amazed at how easily he could change gears without even thinking about it. Every gear change was seamless and smooth. A few hours later, he asked me if I wanted to drive. I admitted that my knowledge of manual cars was minimal to none. He assured me it was alright and I would do just fine. I did not do just fine. For the most part, every time I attempted to shift gears, the entire Jeep would either violently jump or flat out stall. In a few instances, I even tried to shift into the entirely wrong gear. The Jeep under my brother-in-law's control was a smooth and fun driving machine. Under my control, it was out-of-control and dangerous.

The transition statement is comparable to shifting gears in a manual car. The transition should be smooth and seamless. If your transition statement is jarring and unnatural, the prospect will sense the shift and will resist it. Just like the Jeep, a violent jump will alarm the prospect.

The worst thing that can happen is that you stall the process. As I learned from driving the Jeep, once you mess up a gear change (unless you are skilled enough to not panic on the road) you basically have to start all over. This is no different.

The best way to perform a smooth transition is to have a prepared, go-to statement ready to use. This statement should not only be rehearsed, but it should flow naturally from the conversation in the prior step.

Here are a few examples of some great transition statements that you can use, no matter what you sell or what the situation might be:

- "Let me make a recommendation to you."
- "Based on what you told me, I'd like to show you this."
- "I think you will appreciate what we have going on right now."

Notice that each transition statement has the familiar theme of exclusivity for the prospect. Individualizing the transition statement (Let me make a recommendation **to you**) is a subtle way to communicate that what you will be pitching is custom tailored to the individual.

We'll continue with the security example from the prior stops to illustrate how this can work.

> *You:* "Looks like your house is covered with another company. What made you choose them over anyone else?"
>
> *Prospect:* "I'm honestly not too sure. We just picked them because that's what my parents have and they like it."

You: "They have certainly been around for a while here and have a loyal customer base. However, a lot of people I talk to are becoming concerned as to what happens if someone breaks in when they are not home. What is your plan of action in case this happens?"

Prospect: "Well, we usually arm our systems when we leave the house, so the police should be notified if that happens."

You: "Great - arming your system already puts you ahead of what a lot of other folks are doing. However, it seems that more often than not, when people break in they get in and out pretty quickly. By the time the police arrive, they are already gone. Tell me about your current system response rate."

Prospect: "Not too sure. You know, I guess we kind of just hope that they call the police quickly so they can get there in time, but I hear it takes a while."

You: **"That seems like a big what-if, especially when seconds count. You know, based on what you have told me, let me make a recommendation to you."**

The transition is smooth, natural, and customized for the individual prospect. It's important to note that there are certain transition statements that you should attempt to stay away from. One common transition phrase that should be avoided is to ask the prospect if they have heard about your product/service. Very similar to the previous stops, asking a closed-ended question like that can easily backfire on you. If the prospect tells you that they have heard of it and don't like it, your Jeep just stalled and you'll have a hard time getting back in gear. Keep the transition statement customized, natural, and avoid the closed-ended questions.

The why

Earlier in this book, we talked about identifying your *personal why* and your *professional why*. Those things are extremely important to remember during this whole process, but this is where knowing your *professional why* really comes in handy. Just to recap the difference: your *personal why* is essentially your reason for getting up in the morning and going to work every day, while your *professional why* is either your personal reason for selling that particular product/service or your company mission statement/core beliefs. In this section, the *why* that you will want to communicate to the prospect is essentially the reason why your product exists and what purpose it serves, which comes directly from your *professional why*.

You can always incorporate elements of your company's overall mission statement and values in here, but the *why* at this part needs to be specific to the product/service you are selling and the individual you are talking to. For example, my wife and I recently decided to seriously consider buying a home. Being completely new to home-buying, we were a little scared of going through the mortgage process. I have heard horror stories regarding mountains of paperwork and files that needed to be accessed from years back, so we avoided the entire process for a long time. Fortunately, we were approached by a mortgage banker who specialized in first-time homebuyers. The representative I spoke with had a *why* that went something like this:

- "Here, we know that buying a house can be scary, especially if you are a first time buyer. Traditional mortgage service companies can not only be inconvenient for the always-busy modern family, but also complicated to understand. Here, we believe that buying a home should be a stress-free and exciting experience. We offer a service that is both easy to understand and convenient for you."

Again, this is where knowing your company's mission statement, values, and vision all come into play. It also shows the prospect that you stand behind your company and share the same beliefs. This concept goes back to the introduction stop as well, where you proudly stated what company you represent or what product you are selling. This is where that trust in you and in your company will be tested. If you confidently stood behind your brand in the introduction, it will be much more genuine and believable when you bring up the *professional why* in the pitch.

When you talk about your company and what they believe, it shows the prospect that your company is not only listening to the needs of the market, but also doing something different than the rest of the competition. It opens their mind to the idea that your brand truly cares, which will make them much more receptive to the entire pitch.

When you bring up the *why* here, you will want to bring up a couple different truths - stating the current norm, and stating what separates you from the rest.

Stating the current norm

If we look at our example with the mortgage service company, the first part of that was essentially painting the current situation in an overall negative light:

- "Here, we know that buying a house can be scary, especially if you are a first time buyer. Traditional mortgage service companies can not only be inconvenient for the always-busy modern family, but also complicated to understand."

    This accomplished a couple different agendas. The first agenda behind this is to get the prospect (me) to agree that something is wrong with the norm that needs to be fixed. In this case, if I agreed that traditional mortgage companies are inconvenient and complicated, I would be open to what they have to say next about their company.

    The second agenda that should be accomplished is to bring the norm around and customize it for the prospect. Here, they said that the norm was especially complicated and difficult for first time buyers. Being that my wife and I were first-time buyers, we felt more strongly about it and were more than likely agree with them.

    It's important to note here that they did not point out how bad a single competitor is. This could backfire if the prospects have brand loyalty to someone else or if they have had no issues with the competition. You really don't want to make the prospect feel stupid or silly for using a different company. That's why it's a better idea to use a blanket statement that paints the norm in an overall negative light.

<u>Stating how you fix the norm</u>

The next step here would be to essentially state how your company or product fixes the norm. This is the place where you'll want to remember your *professional why* - if you can recall and state what your company fundamentally believes in terms of their overall mission, you'll certainly get the attention of the prospect here.

Let's take a look at the previous example, with the appropriate section bolded:

- "Here, we know that buying a house can be scary, especially if you are a first time buyer. Traditional mortgage service companies can not only be inconvenient for the always-busy modern family, but also complicated to understand. **Here, we believe that buying a home should be a stress-free and exciting experience. We offer a service that is both easy to understand and convenient for you.**"

Notice how they stated that "We believe" and "We offer." They did not state that "My company believes that…" or "The corporation offers…" This is important because, as we mentioned previously in this book, it's imperative to display a unified front throughout the entire process. In the prospect's eyes, you should be a natural extension of the company that you represent. By saying "We believe…," you are demonstrating that you are not only a professional representative of the company, but that you believe the same things and have the same mission that the company has. As stated before, this is important in building and maintaining trust.

Also note that they gave a simple and broad overview of how they fix the norm. They did not 'name the puppy' and go over all the details of the company or all the details of every product. At this point in the pitch, you want to have the prospect's interest peaked. They should be literally leaning in to hear what you have to say next. Whatever you say next will likely resonate with the prospect. For example, if you suddenly begin to discuss the long history of your company, the prospect will focus their full attention on that, and not the product.

That's why your next step in the pitch should be something that every salesperson in the world is trained on, every business school student is taught, and what every prospect is waiting for: the features and benefits of the product/service itself.

Let's finish off the *why* with our security example:

- "Here, we know that security coverage can be pricey and unreliable. Traditional security companies can charge you whatever they want while providing substandard services. **Here, we believe that every family has the right to feel safe and secure, regardless of budget. We offer a service that is both reasonably priced and highly reliable.**"

The features, advantages, and benefits

Features, advantages, and benefits, also known as FAB, are the meat & potatoes of every salesperson's pitch. If we were on our road trip, the features, advantages, and benefits portion of the pitch would be your steering wheel. This is the section of your pitch where you have the power to steer the prospect's attention to whatever you want. Whatever you decide to talk about in this section will be the deciding factor in the mind of the prospect.

Rather than talking more about your *company why* or your *product why*, this section is all about describing your product/service in detail to the prospect. This is where your technical knowledge comes into play. Ideally, you should receive training on your product/service before you speak to a prospect. Most salespeople are heavily trained on the features, advantages, and benefits of their product/service directly from their company during their onboarding phase. As a sales professional of the company, the expectation is that you are able to be an expert in whatever it is that you sell. It's difficult to imagine a scenario where a company will not conduct proper training, but if this is ever the case, you will want to do as much research as you can on your product/service and become an expert at it. Even if your company does train you, it never hurts to gather as much information about your product as possible so you can relay that information to your prospects.

The kicker here is that when presented at face value, prospects generally will not care about your product/service, no matter what it is. For example, let's go back to our ongoing example with the security company.

- "Here, we have the premium all-inclusive security package that retails for only about $50/month. It should fit all your needs!"

If you approach the prospect and your product pitch is something like that, they probably won't be inclined to buy it from you because you did not describe any of the features, advantages, or benefits of the premium all-inclusive package. Although you did say that it fits all of their needs, without knowing what exactly comes with that package how will they decide if it's a good value for them or not? You essentially are putting a price tag on a service that the prospect knows nothing about. It puts the prospect in a situation where they will make a decision without any information, which will ultimately result in less closed sales and more rescissions. This is why it's important to know what the features, advantages, and benefits are.

Features

Your product/service *features* can be easily described as the physical characteristics or facts about your product/service. The features are usually specific and describe the appearance and components of whatever it is that you are selling. The features are often the easiest to describe because they are basic cold hard facts that can easily be listed on a sheet of paper.

After my wife and I talked to the mortgage banker, we decided to go forward with purchasing our first home together. After selecting our budget and going through the financing approval phase we set out to find a forever home. As all house-hunters know, the search can be overwhelming, especially when presented with a barrage of different options. One thing that we did notice was that every real estate information sheet listed the house features in a bullet-list format. Once we found a house that we were interested in, our real estate agent handed us a sheet of paper with the following features listed:

- Type: Single Family
- Year Built: 2015
- Heating: Heat pump
- Windows: Eco-Glazed Glass
- Water: City source
- Parking: 2 car garage detached
- Bedrooms: 3
- Bathrooms: 3
- Basement: None
- Roof type: Asphalt

- Exterior: Vinyl
- Floor size: 1,944 sq. ft.
- Lot size: 8,405 sq. ft.
- Flooring: Hardwood/Carpet

All of these were facts and features about the home that we were interested in. This is all extremely important information to know as a potential buyer. Without this information, we would not be able to make a purchasing decision at all, nor would we want to.

It does not matter if you are selling homes, cars, timeshare, security systems, etc. All products/services have a list of facts and features that must be presented to the prospect. While having all the facts and features of a product is important, as a salesperson you'll want to understand what your prospect is looking for and direct them to those particular features. For example, our real estate agent knew (from her own *Discovering a Need* step) that we were looking for a house that had three bedrooms, had at least 1,600 sq. ft. of living space, and had a decent sized yard for our two dogs. When this house was presented to us, she directed our attention to those features because that's what we were looking for specifically.

Features are also good to use when comparing two products/services with the prospect. Going back to the real estate example, our realtor would often show us three or more homes at once, all side-by-side with the facts and features listed accordingly. From there, we were able to get a pretty good idea of what houses we wanted to see and which ones we wanted to pass up.

Let's go back to the security example that we have been using so far in this book. If you are presenting the premium package to a prospect you will want to focus on the facts and features that are found within that package:

- Burglar monitoring
- Smoke and fire monitoring
- Flood monitoring
- Remote arm and disarm
- Video surveillance with two cameras
- Video doorbell that alerts your phone when someone is at your front door
- Instant communication to police
- 24 hour monitoring
- Remote control of lights
- Remote locking and unlocking of all doors
- 100% instant accessibility via the free app

Listing the features allows the prospect to get a high-level overview of the basic facts surrounding your product/service. Not only do you simply want to list them, but you will want to divert the prospect's attention on those features that are important to them (which you should know from your *Discovering a Need* stop). As we know, our prospect is interested in the burglar monitoring system, the 24 hour monitoring, instant accessibility via the app, and the instant communication to police feature. When presenting these features to the prospect a great way to divert their attention to those features is to simply remind them of what their product needs are.

- "Let me show you our premium package. Based on what you told me, this package has everything that your family needs. Of course, it comes with burglar monitoring, 24 hour monitoring, and instant communication with the police. It also comes with several other components that I would recommend - fire, smoke, and flood monitoring, remote arm and disarm control, remote control of your lights, and remote locking and unlocking of your doors. My favorite component is the free app. If you are ever in a position where you are not home, this app will alert you when someone is at your front door."

All we did here was list the product facts behind the premium all-inclusive package. Again, these are the features that can be easily described because they are the core components of the product and service. However, just listing off all the facts and features is not enough to build value in the prospect. Otherwise, all we would have to do would be to hand out fliers to prospects that listed all the features on them. While this can work in some instances, it's important for us to build value by describing the features in a way that the prospect can relate to, which brings us to the next part: the advantages.

Advantages

The *advantages* can be easily defined as what the features can actually do in terms of functionality. This is different from the listed features themselves in the sense that the features are simply facts and data about the product/service. If you describe how the features work and what they can do, that's describing the advantages of that feature.

Going back to the previous example of my wife and I looking for a house to purchase, one of the features of the house that we were interested in was the eco-glazed windows. That's a simple *feature* of the house - the windows have a glaze on them that makes them environmentally friendlier. The *advantage* of the windows is that they are coated with a special material that is better at inhibiting heat transfer, which means that they are better at keeping the temperature constant in the room. That's the advantage of having the eco-glaze rather than a regular double-pane window.

Mechanically, this looks like this:

- The feature was: eco-glazed windows.
- The advantage was: windows that inhibit heat transfer, which allows for the room to be better at holding the temperature.

Advantages essentially describe why the product or service is functionally superior. This is where your technical knowledge comes in handy. This can be used in either a business-to-business (B2B) or a business-to-consumer (B2C) setting too. If, for example, let's imagine that you are a B2B salesperson and are selling your manufacturing services to a purchaser from a large company. You know that one of the features that you can offer is the fact that your company has the most efficient manufacturing system in the industry and is open 24/7. The advantage of the system is that it takes full advantage of economies of scale by using state-of-the-art machines that can manufacture goods at a much more demanding pace in a manner that is much more reliable.

Again, this looks like:

- The feature was: an efficient manufacturing system.
- The advantage was: new machines that are faster and more reliable.

Let's revisit the security example again. As we know, our list of features included 24 hour monitoring as one of the features that we identified as important to the prospect. The advantage of that service is that with a fully staffed 24-

hour monitoring room, a real person will always be ready to help and provide instant communication to the police and the residents if necessary, regardless of the time of day.

- The feature was: 24 hour monitoring.
- The advantage was: the fully staffed monitoring room with real people who are always on standby to help.

Conversationally, we can add the advantages in when describing the features.

- "Let me show you our premium package. Based on what you told me, this package has everything that your family needs. Of course, it comes with burglar monitoring, 24 hour monitoring, and instant communication with the police. **We have a fully staffed secure monitoring facility with real people who are on standby to help.** It also comes with several other components that I would recommend - fire, smoke, and flood monitoring, remote arm and disarm control, remote control of your lights, and remote locking and unlocking of your doors. My favorite component is the free app. If you are ever in a position where you are not home, this app will alert you when someone is at your front door."

Advantages are important because they give real meaning to the features. Had my realtor not described the advantages of the eco-glazed windows, I never would have known, so it would have seemed like a non-important element to the house. Now, I have a greater appreciation for the house in general.

Unfortunately, just listing the advantages is still not enough to build value with the prospect. After all, the whole idea behind the pitch is to make your product relevant to the prospect. Features are simple meaningless facts about the product. Advantages give the features meaning, but not relevance to the prospect individually. This is why the next step is so crucial. Without it, prospects will have a difficult time understanding why they need to purchase your product/service at all.

Benefits

Benefits can be defined as the relevance of the advantages to that prospect individually. The benefit of the product/service is where you will really drive the point home for your prospects and where you will build enough value to make a sale happen. As we have discussed earlier in this book, making your presentation exclusive for the prospect is one of the best ways that you can build trust and value. This is where that concept will really be the difference between a successful sales call and one that is not. At the end of the day, if a prospect does not feel like your product/service is relevant to them, they will have no need to purchase it. If they do feel it is relevant to them and can indeed help them, they have a much stronger likelihood of saying "yes" to you. This part is where you will make it relevant.

To keep it consistent with this section, let's continue with the house example. At this point in the discussion, my real estate agent gave me the feature that the windows were ecologically friendly. She told me that the advantage was that it could inhibit heat transfer more efficiently than regular windows. The main benefit to me individually was that my HVAC would use significantly less energy, which translates to significant direct financial savings for me personally.

- The feature was: eco-glazed windows.
- The advantage was: windows that inhibit heat transfer, which allows for the room to be better at holding the temperature.
- The benefit was: our HVAC system uses less energy to heat/cool the house, which means I save a lot of money every month on energy bills.

For me, this benefit was amazingly important. We live in a climate where our energy bills are often ridiculously expensive. This benefit, which started off as a simple feature, turned into a major selling point for me. This is why explaining the benefits are so important. It makes the features and advantages relevant to the prospect.

Looking back at the B2B example again, where we are selling our manufacturing services to a prospect. We told the prospect that a feature was that we had the most efficient operating system in the industry. Our machines are brand new and can manufacture at a more demanding pace while being reliable. The benefit to that prospect individually is that the product will be 25% less expensive than their current supplier, which means they now have the freedom to keep a large margin or discount their prices.

- The feature was: an efficient manufacturing system.
- The advantage was: new machines that are faster and more reliable.
- The benefit was: a 25% less expensive yet identical product and also having the freedom to either make 25% more money or discount their prices.

Benefits make it real. Benefits make your product/service important. It's worth noting that if you have not properly completed the *Discovering a Need* stop, this will be significantly more difficult. If you remember, that's the stop where the prospect tells us what their problems & needs are. The benefits section is where you can match your product/service up **exactly** to those problems & needs.

For the last example here, let's go back to the security example. Of course, the feature that we are choosing to emphasize with the prospect is the 24 hour monitoring. The advantage is that we have a fully staffed 24-hour monitoring room with real people who are always on standby to help. The benefit here for the prospect individually would be that the staff would notify the prospect and police of any suspicious activity right away, regardless of the time of day. Police would get notified 2x faster than the current methods, and will therefore arrive at the scene much faster. With the constant monitoring, the prospect can rest easy knowing that their house will be protected all the time.

- The feature was: 24 hour monitoring.
- The advantage was: the fully staffed monitoring room with real people who are always on standby to help.
- The benefit was: the staff would notify the prospect and police of any suspicious activity right away, regardless of the time of day. Police would get notified 2x faster than the current methods.

Benefits build value. Without them, prospects will have a difficult time bridging the gap between the advantages and why they should buy it. In the next step, we will see how we can put all this together in a conversational format to form powerful features, advantages, and benefits statements that will compel the prospect to purchase.

FAB/BAF statements

It's not enough just to rattle off features, advantages, and benefits to prospects in a boring manner. It's important to have a series of power statements for each feature that you want to present to the prospect. These statements should be able to encapsulate a product/service's technical characteristics (features), what the characteristic can do (advantages) and why it's perfect for that individual prospect (benefits).

When presenting the features, advantages, and benefits in sentence form, you can either give the prospect a FAB statement or a BAF statement. Both statements accomplish the same thing and both sentences have the exact same meaning, we just reverse the order of the features, advantages, and benefits.

Let's go back to the example of us looking at the house with the eco-friendly windows.

FAB (Features, Advantages, Benefits)

- "Mr. and Mrs. Karaman, one of the features of this particular house is that it has eco-glazed windows. The windows are actually coated with this really neat special ecologically-friendly material that better inhibits heat transfer than regular window panes, which allows the room to stay colder in the summer and hotter in the winter. This means that your HVAC system won't have to work has hard, which means you will saving a ton of money on energy bills."

As we can see, the FAB statement perfectly describes the feature, what the advantage is, and why it benefits me personally.

BAF (Benefits, Advantages, Features)

You don't have to describe features strictly with the FAB formula. Depending on what you sell, you can switch the order around to first discuss the benefits, then the advantages, and finish off with the actual feature. This might sound backwards and might sound a little awkward, but it can work extremely effectively because it serves as a buildup for the feature itself. When a prospect knows the benefit first, they will be subconsciously curious to hear what the feature is.

Here's how it would look with the case for our windows:

- "Mr. and Mrs. Karaman, one of the best parts about this house is that it's economically efficient in terms of energy. The HVAC system doesn't have to work as hard to maintain the temperature, so you save a ton of money on energy costs. The windows are specially designed to inhibit heat transfer better than regular paned windows, so your house will stay cold in the summer and hot in the winter. They are covered in a really neat ecologically-friendly glaze, so you'll notice a green tint when the sun hits it just right."

Whichever method you decide to use, you'll accomplish the same goal of describing the features in a rich, descriptive, and enticing way. The prospects will start to see that they really can benefit from your product/service because we made all the features specialized to them individually. You should use whichever one 'feels' better for you to avoid any awkwardness in your pitch. Me personally, I'm a fan of the FAB statements.

It's important to note that you should not be listing 100% of your features like this. While you should absolutely disclose all features to your prospect, you should only use the FAB statements for the ones that are relevant to the prospect. For example - the supplier might primarily care about the fact that his competitor is beating him on cost, so he would be greatly interested in our operations model.

- "Mr. Smith, one useful element about our manufacturing plant is that we have the most efficient operations system in the industry. All of our machines are brand new and our plant is running 24/7, which means we can produce and distribute an identical product at a lower cost to you. This means that you will be able to sell this same product at a 25% lower cost. You'll have the freedom to either make 25% more money or lower your prices."

Of course, this would have all been uncovered in the *Discovering a Need* stop, so you should not have to guess as to which feature you should emphasize. If you start to describe a feature that the prospect ultimately does not care about, you will not only gain no traction, but you'll actually hurt your progress. The prospect might feel misunderstood and will probably become irritated. Worse - the prospect thinks that you were not even listening to them and becomes frustrated at you and your brand. This is why it's extremely important to not skip stops and try a shortcut. A lot of people will oftentimes try to expedite the process and jump straight from *Rapport Building* to this stop. Without discovering a need first, you'll be pitching features that don't make sense to the prospect. Do that and you risk the entire road trip falling apart.

To finish the illustration, let's finish off with the Safe Security FAB statement regarding the video surveillance:

- "Mr. Jones, one of the most important features we have in this package is our 24 hour monitoring service. We have a room of fully staffed and real associates ready to help at a moment's notice. If they notice any burglar activity or if the alarm is sounded, we will notify both you and the police at the same time. Police will get notified two times faster and will arrive at your house much quicker. You'll never have to worry about being on your own in an emergency - someone will always be there to help you regardless of the time or day and we will be there to help immediately."

The proof

Once you describe the features, advantages, and benefits of your product/service, you will instinctively feel like it's time to close the prospect. After all, if the prospect sees the features as real benefits to them individually, why would we not want to close right away?

While the prospect might truly understand the benefits to them, there will still be a little hint of doubt in you and in your product. Making a purchase can often be some of the most inquisitive times in someone's life, especially if it's a large purchase. Just hearing your features, advantages, and benefits won't be enough to fully convince someone to dive right in and become an advocate for your product/service. People ultimately want proof. They want reassurance that they made the correct choice. They want to feel like people in similar situations have benefited from this. That's why we have this next step - to serve as proof for the prospect.

Don't think that just because you have great rapport with the prospect and have built a high level of trust that they will trust your product/service to do as promised. Proof is a powerful idea that will only serve to benefit you. You should always have a way to illustrate this for the prospect, even if they look like they are ready to buy. Nobody (to my knowledge) has ever changed their mind about buying at the last minute because the sales representative offered too much proof of the product/service working.

Proving your product works can be done in a number of different ways.

Offering tangible evidence

One of the easiest ways that you can show proof of your product/service working is to offer some form of tangible evidence to the prospect. Essentially, presenting them with real, visual information that proves your point. This is by far the easiest way to build that final level of trust with the prospect. After all, seeing is believing.

Tangible evidence can be anything that the prospect can look at and see with their own two eyes. Not only does it affirm that the product works, but it helps the prospect really understand the benefits. Once they visualize the proof, it makes it even more real for them.

Examples of evidence includes any and all of the following:

- Charts
- Graphs
- A live demonstration
- Video documentation
- Statistics
- Testimonials
- Pictures

Whichever form you decide to use, make sure you fully describe the evidence to the prospect. If my realtor had shown me a complicated diagram about the eco-friendly windows without describing what it was, I would have seen little value in the proof. Sometimes, proof can be complicated for the prospect to fully understand at first glance. Comprehensive data sheets and charts are examples of complicated proof that need to be described in detail. This is not a new concept - that's why lawyers describe evidence in court. They want to make sure the jury fully understands the evidence. The same principle applies here.

Let's revisit the B2B example from the last step. If we had just presented our FAB statement regarding the highly efficient manufacturing process that we employ, our proof could be a graph showing the manufacturing capabilities of our machines with a corresponding economy of scale diagram. This is complicated at first glance, but when we describe it to the prospect, it becomes more understandable.

- "Mr. Smith, one useful element about our manufacturing plant is that we have the most efficient operations system in the industry. All of our machines are brand new and our plant is running 24/7, which means we can produce and distribute an identical product at a lower cost to you. This means that you will be able to sell this same product at a 25% lower cost. You'll have the freedom to either make 25% more money or lower your prices. **Here is a graph that shows our production capabilities. With basic sheet metal products, we can produce at nearly 2x the rate of the competition. The chart here shows how much money you would save per order by using our process here**."

While the proof might be complex and complicated, describing it in easy-to-understand language will help the prospect easier see the value in your product/service. Let's go back to the security example. We established that the benefit was that we would instantly communicate any signs of danger to both the prospect and police, so ultimately the police would respond twice as fast to an incident. The proof that we can offer would potentially be hard data of our police response rates in comparison to the industry average. We could have arrival time statistics displayed in a chart. The way we would describe this proof to the prospect would look something like this:

- "Mr. Jones, one of the most important features we have in this package is our 24 hour monitoring service. We have a room of fully staffed and real associates ready to help at a moment's notice. If they notice any burglar activity or if the alarm is sounded, we will notify both you and the police at the same time. Police will get notified two times faster and will arrive at your house much quicker. You'll never have to worry about being on your own in an emergency - someone will always be there to help you regardless of the time or day and we will be there to help immediately. **I have this graph that shows police response rates between us and the industry average, which includes our competition. As you can see, our response rate is half of the average. We measure our own times too - we have never had a response time that exceeded the average. On our worst day, we still beat the competition.**"

Just like with every other step, notice that we are using rich and descriptive language. We are showcasing our product in the very best light. If police response rate was one of the key issues with our prospect (in this case, it was), how could they possibly deny that is a major benefit to them? This could trigger a 'switch' in the mind of the prospect that our security services really are perfect for them.

Telling a 3rd party story

Physical proof will always remain one of the most effective ways to show proof to a prospect. Another fantastic way you can prove your point is to tell the prospect a 3rd party story about a similar prospect that has success with your product/service. Telling stories are most beneficial to those who do not have any tangible proof available. Rather than showing visual proof, you are telling a true story about a similar prospect that used your product/service and had success with it.

Remember, people look for proof because they want reassurance that they made the correct choice. They want to feel like people in similar situations have benefited from whatever it is they are buying. You have most definitely done this exercise without even realizing it. We consumers do that all the time. Have you ever looked at a website for user reviews before or after a purchase? Those sites allow for real people, just like you, to submit feedback on restaurants, activities, and businesses. Websites like that are so popular because people want to know other people's experiences with the brand. Personally, I use it all the time when looking for new restaurants. Often times, I make my decision purely based on the feedback from others. Peer assurance is a powerful tool and can be just as effective as tangible proof.

If you work in an industry that has a large online review presence, you can easily reference the reviews. While this borders on the line of tangible evidence, it can still be used to tell the story. In most cases where there is not a large online presence, your stories will revolve around past customers who were in situations very similar to that of your prospects. You can look back on past experiences of your own, or past experiences of the brand itself, whichever situation is more relevant.

Storytelling is an art. You have to tell a story that is not only entertaining, but valuable in the eyes of the prospect. When telling a story, you'll want to remember a couple of points:

- Storytelling is only as valuable as it is relevant, meaning that if you tell a story that the prospect has no connection with, they will be even more tuned out by the end of it. Just like with the evidence, you want your story to be exclusive to the prospect. While you are telling a story about someone else, the situation should mirror the prospect's. The end result of the story should be the same benefit that the prospect is hoping to see from your product.

- Any good storyteller is good at using words to illustrate their story. By painting the picture, it does not leave the story up to interpretation for the prospect. One of my favorite examples has nothing to do with sales, but it is relevant here. In J. R. R. Tolkien's *Lord of the Rings* books, he painted such a profound and clear picture of Middle-Earth and the characters. When reading it, you have a perfect idea of what the environment looks like. This was verified by everybody when the movies came out – what I viewed on the big screen was already in my head. You want to accomplish the same thing with your story

- Every story has a problem and a solution. That's why people listen to stories; they want to hear how the problem was solved. Every book that was ever authored follows the same formula and your story in sales should do the same. As mentioned above, you want to have a problem that is relevant to your prospect, then show how it was solved with your product. If you are able to do this, it shows that your product or service is capable of solving real problems and should be trusted.

For example, my wife and I were excited about saving energy with the new windows because it would save us money while being green. A 3rd party story should be revolving around similar buyers who moved into a house with that style of windows and only pays $60/month in the summer on electricity. In the case of the B2B salesperson, the 3rd party might revolve around a similar distributor who was able to lower the price in his market and capture 30% more customers than before.

Here is an example of an engaging and effective 3rd party story that we might tell to the prospect that is looking at our premium security package:

- "Mr. Jones, one of the most important features we have in this package is our 24 hour monitoring service. We have a room of fully staffed and real associates ready to help at a moment's notice. If they notice any burglar activity or if the alarm is sounded, we will notify both you and the police at the same time. Police will get notified two times faster and will arrive at your house much quicker. You'll never have to worry about being on your own in an emergency - someone will always be there to help you regardless of the time or day and we will be there to help immediately. **A few months ago, my neighbor was out of town on business. His wife and child were home by themselves. Late at night, someone tried to gain entrance through a window with a crowbar. We caught it within seconds and the police were out there soon after. They were able to catch the suspect and nobody was hurt. My neighborhood is much safer now."**

Even if you DO have tangible evidence, don't write 3rd party stories off. You can certainly tell stories in place of hard evidence, but it's just as effective if it's used in conjunction with the hard evidence. It only gives you a stronger position of proof, which is the key in establishing trust.

- "Mr. Jones, one of the most important features we have in this package is our 24 hour monitoring service. We have a room of fully staffed and real associates ready to help at a moment's notice. If they notice any burglar activity or if the alarm is sounded, we will notify both you and the police at the same time. Police will get notified two times faster and will arrive at your house much quicker. You'll never have to worry about being on your own in an emergency - someone will always be there to help you regardless of the time or day and we will be there to help immediately. I have this graph that shows police response rates between us and the industry average, which includes our competition. As you can see, our response rate is half of the average. We measure our own times too - we have never had a response time that exceeded the average. On our worst day, we still beat the competition. **A few months ago, my neighbor was out of town on business. His wife and child were home by themselves. Late at night, someone tried to gain entrance through a window with a crowbar. We caught it within seconds and the police were out there soon after. They were able to catch the suspect and nobody was hurt. My neighborhood is much safer now."**

While it might seem excessive on paper to offer both styles of proof, it will be more natural sounding when spoken to the prospect. Stories serve as an easy way to show the prospect that their peers have enjoyed success with the product/service.

Keep it ethical

When it comes to proof (or anything else in business for that matter), honesty is always the best policy. You should never attempt to forge proof. This is important because lying not only violates sales ethics, but also destroys your credibility too. Worse - lying puts your entire brand image at risk.

You should never attempt to deceive a prospect by showing them fake or meaningless evidence. Such tactics might result in a short-term sale but doing so inhibits the possibility of a long-term loyal prospect. If discovered by the prospect that you have deceived them in any way the level of trust that you worked so hard to build will be destroyed. Once that trust is gone, making another sale and having sustained business success become very difficult. You should only be presenting physical evidence that is meaningful, helpful, and actually serves as real proof.

The same principle applies when telling stories. It's pretty easy to be caught in a lie. If you lie about a story, it won't have the same impact on the prospect because they will be able to sense that you are not 100% invested in it. Your passions will not show in a fake story, so only tell true ones. Not to mention - if you start to make up stories to your prospects, you run the risk of contradicting yourself somewhere on accident. Lying in general is a very poor way to earn business. Your reputation precedes you, so if you develop a reputation for making up stories you will be constantly fighting an uphill battle with every prospect interaction.

At the end of the day make sure your proof shows undeniable evidence of your product/service working. If you have physical proof, ensure that it is legitimate and meaningful evidence. Don't just show prospects random graphs and charts that don't actually mean anything. If you are telling stories, don't lie and make up scenarios.

At this point, we have already transitioned into business mode, shared our *whys*, described the features, advantages, and benefits to the prospect, and proved that our security system is truly superior to the competition with tangible evidence and a story. You might want to close the prospect right now, but we still have one more thing to accomplish. While we have successfully built up *value* to the prospect, we have not yet put a *price* on that value.

The price

We have just spent the past hundred pages talking about how to build value. While each stop might be labelled differently, they all serve to accomplish one similar goal: to build value in the eyes of the prospect. In the *Introduce Yourself* and *Rapport Building* stops, you build value in yourself and the brand. In the *Discovering a Need* stop and so far in this stop, we have been building value in the product/service. Now, we have to put a price on that service - meaning we have to tell the prospect how much it costs.

A lot of people are almost afraid to talk about price. It can be one of the most delicate portions of your sales pitch but talking about price is nothing you should be afraid of. The prospect already knows that your product/service is not free. Not to mention, you hopefully just built up a tremendous amount of value, so when they see or hear the price, they should not be shocked. This section is not about actually setting the price. Price setting strategies and research can fill up an entire book by itself. Not to mention, setting the original price is something that most salespeople don't have any control over. It is what it is. Your job is to build the right amount of value for the prospect so that the price makes sense for them. You have to present the price in a way where the prospect wins because the benefits that they are getting are worth more than the cost, regardless of what that cost may be.

If you are selling products that are priced lower than the competition, don't think that price alone can always close a sale. If you don't build enough value before presenting the price, the prospect might think that you have a lower quality product/service and will assume that your product will have less benefit to them. That's why it's important to go through the previous steps in this stop before talking about price, even if it's lower than the competition.

The same idea applies to products/services that are priced at a premium, meaning that they are more expensive than the competition. If you don't build enough value in the benefits, prospects will be unable to rationalize the higher price. While they might make the assumption that it's higher quality because of the premium price, not understanding what the premium benefits actually are might prevent them from purchasing.

The worst thing that you can do is simply not talk about the price. Like we said before, prospects understand that your product/service isn't free. They know that it costs *something.* If you skip over the price and try to close the prospect first, they will become suspicious that you are hiding something. Trust will erode and you're entire road trip can come to a sudden halt.

That being said, just blurting out the price to the prospect is not an effective way to communicate the cost either. The way that you present the price will ultimately be dependent on your specific strategy. Much like every element in this stop so far, price has to be pitched in a way that benefits that individual prospect. This is why I included price in the *Pitch* stop, rather than the *Close* stop. A lot of people want to lump the price into the close. While you can indeed use the price as a closing method (we'll talk about how we can do this in the next stop), we have to remember that the price is tied to the product. The value is tied in with the product - so when we close the prospect, we are closing on both the *product* and the *price*.

Be confident

The first thing to remember when talking about price is to never be apologetic. Whether your product/service is priced at a premium or at a discount, you should always say your price with confidence and assurance. The less confident you are with your price, the more skeptical the prospect will become. Your product/service is priced at the perceived value. If you just spent the last twenty minutes building that value up, don't tear it back down by being apologetic for the price.

If the prospect even gets a hint of resistance from you regarding what the cost is, they might feel like *you* believe that the price is somehow unfair. If the prospect thinks that you do not agree with the price, why would they themselves pay it? Remember, your price is tied in with the product, so you have to maintain the same confidence in your price as your product itself.

The best way you can confidently state the price is to remember the same principles that are found at stop 1. Back when we were introducing ourselves, we went over the 3 E's. The 3 E's help us gain the attention of the prospect and focus their attention on us. In this case, rather than focusing their attention on us, we want to direct their attention on not only the price, but the value.

The Pitch

- Energy: If you remember, having positive energy means displaying positive and open body language. Sit/stand up straight, make eye contact, and smile. This will show the prospect that you are confident in the price and have nothing to be ashamed about.
- Excitement: This is found in the tone of your voice, which represents your general disposition towards the price. When you communicate the price to a prospect, you shouldn't quietly whisper or mumble it. Your tone of voice has to be upbeat and positive. The more positive you are about the price, the more "right" it will seem.
- Enthusiasm: To be enthusiastic is to have rich and descriptive language. Rather than saying something "costs $500," you can say that "the total investment will be $500." We will elaborate about how to describe the price further in the next section. Essentially, your verbiage surrounding the price has to be positive as well.

Taking advantage of the 3 E's is a way you can confidently pitch your price to a prospect. Price should not be something you are afraid of. If you have built up the right level of value, the price should make sense in the mind of the prospect. It should also make sense in your own mind as well. Confidence is a great way to communicate that you agree with the price and stand by it.

Use positive language

When we use positive language we are building something up with our choice of words. Building value by describing the product with strong and persuasive FAB statements is a way we use positive language to communicate our point.

For example, when we were talking about my wife and I purchasing our home, our realtor showed us the eco-windows by using various terms such as "investment" and "savings." Had she said something negative, such as "expensive," we would have been focused on the price of it, not the benefits or the value. Essentially, positive language focused our attention from one way of looking at the windows (expensive and unnecessary) to something else entirely (efficient and money-saving). It's a way to pitch the features, advantages, and benefits and paint them all in the best light possible.

When you are discussing price, your verbiage is important because you can either focus the attention of the prospect on the negative (overpriced/cheap) or the positive (absolutely worth it/a great value). The way you describe the price is ultimately the way the prospect will view it:

Common Pricing Terms	Positive Language
"This service costs $600/year."	"Your total investment will be $600/year."
"The low-cost option is $25/month."	"At $25/month, this is the most cost-effective opportunity."
"Our highest tiered service is priced at $50/month."	"Our highest quality of service is just $50/month."
"Our introductory discount is 20% off for the first year, and then jumps up the normal price after that."	"As a new customer, we'll discount your investment 20%. After a year, we'll return it to normal."

You'll notice that we changed a few words around in each column. The column on the left represents common phrases that most salespeople say. The column on the right represents the same statements, but said in positive language by a master salesperson. Rather than focusing on the words "cost" and "price," we focused on "investment" and "opportunity."

We also referred to the low-cost option as "cost-effective." When people hear "low-cost," they might automatically think that the quality is bad and should be avoided. The same applies if they hear the word "cheap." Nobody really wants to buy a low quality cheap item that has no value to them - they want the most bang for their buck. When talking about prices that are heavily discounted or lower than the competition, focus on the following words:

- Economical
- Cost-Effective
- Inexpensive
- Highest valued
- Competitive
- Reasonable
- Budget

Never use the words "cheap," "low-cost," "rock-bottom." or any other phrase that might indicate a poor level of service/quality. When I was in college, my food budget was next to nothing. One night, a group of my friends and I were in our apartment studying for a marketing exam. It was a late night and we were all getting hungry, so I decided to make some ramen noodles for myself. My friend started to make fun my diet and the quality of the noodles, calling them "cheap" and "terrible."

I laughed and said "No, they are the *most economical and cost-effective* way to eat." That's how you effectively describe something inexpensive with positive language.

So far in this Safe Security example that we have been constantly using throughout this book, we have been pitching the higher cost premium package. We will go over how to pitch the high-cost package later - for the sake of this current section, we'll pretend that we are pitching the low-cost budget package. Here is an example to illustrate positive language surrounding a discounted item:

- "This is our most **cost-effective** opportunity. It's designed to be **economical,** yet we wanted to maintain our level of commitment to you, which means that you will be completely covered in case of burglary or fire at a **less expensive** price. Maintaining the 24 hour monitoring service, the **investment** on this is **extremely reasonable** - only $25/month for peace of mind and to never be alone when an emergency happens."

Here, we took the lowest-priced option and by simply using some positive language, transformed it to a fantastic bargain that delivers high value at a low cost.

On the flip side, let's say that we are selling an expensive, premium product/service. If you are selling a high-priced item, you have the task of building up the perceived value in the mind of the prospect to match the premium price. If you can do this successfully, you should not be afraid to state the price.

As a freshman student at Purdue, I was in desperate need for a new laptop computer. The one I was previously using was several years old. It was stepped on, dropped, and was even spilled on during a party. When I decided I was going to buy a new one, I instantly went looking for the most inexpensive model I could find. When I asked for advice from one of my friends they told me that "I need to go with the newest model. It's a powerful, high quality, premium laptop that will last forever. They run about $1,000, but they are completely worth it."

Notice that he did not seem apologetic for the high price - he stood behind it and was confident that the price of the laptop matched the value and benefits of using it. Again, the way you present the price needs to be in positive/descriptive language. Rather than using the phrases "most expensive" and "high cost," try using the following words:

- Premium
- Highest quality
- Valuable
- Upscale
- Platinum
- Exclusive

All of these words are essentially stating that the product/service is a top-tiered product that is at a premium because the quality is so high. While using these words also add to the value of the price, it's important to stress to the prospect the benefits of the high cost option. Here would be a good example of positive language surrounding our top-tiered security package:

- "Let me show you our **premium** package. This is by far our **highest quality** of service. It comes with all the important features that we discussed before plus a lifetime satisfaction guarantee. Your investment would only be $50/month for the **best** security services in town. You will never feel unsafe again."

There is nothing apologetic about that. We confidently presented our premium package, communicated the value of our service, and firmly stated our price in a manner that shows confidence and trust.

Make it personal

Just like with the FAB statements, you have to remind the prospect that your product/service is perfect for them individually. You might be thinking that it's slightly overkill to emphasize it again. I would disagree - the more we are able to connect the prospect to our product/service, the better off we will be.

We already went through the efforts to describe all the features, advantages, and benefits to the prospect individually, so we really do not have to reiterate every point. A simple reminder that our product/service is *great for them* will do the job:

- **"Based on what you told me, here is my recommendation.** This is our most **cost-effective** opportunity. It's designed to be **economical,** yet we wanted to maintain our level of commitment to you, which means that you will be completely covered in case of burglary or fire at a **less expensive** price. Maintaining the 24 hour monitoring service, the **investment** on this is **extremely reasonable** - only $25/month for peace of mind and to never be alone when an emergency happens. **I think this is perfect for your family and your wallet."**

We used two simple sentences to show the prospect that we are individualizing our recommendation to them personally. If a prospect feels like you have listened to their concerns and are trying to best fix their needs, they will accept whatever your recommendation is. Personalizing your pricing pitch is just another way to make the prospect feel important and valued.

- "**Let me recommend this package to you because I feel it will fit your needs perfectly**. This is our **premium** package. This is by far our **highest quality** of service. It comes with all the important features that we discussed before plus a lifetime satisfaction guarantee. Your investment would only be $50/month for the **best** security services in town. You will never feel unsafe again. **Based on what you told me, this would be the best option for your family**."

All you need is a simple reminder that your product/service is best suited for them and their situation. Again, you can only know this if you have done the proper work in the *Discovering a Need* step. This is another reason why you should not be skipping stops - if you fail to discover a prospect need or a problem and end up pitching a feature that the prospect doesn't care about, your recommendation might come off as high-pressured and bogus.

A word on price negotiation

Some salespeople work at companies and industries that not only allow for negotiation, but almost encourage it. A lot of people buy cars from dealerships and car lots with the expectation that they will not be paying the full sticker price. Here's the thing - if a prospect responds to your price statement with a counteroffer (meaning they wish to negotiate), the proper response would fall in the next stop - *The Close*. A lot of people assume that negotiating should be categorized with price, but remember that if a prospect responds with a counter offer, they are assigning their own value to your product/service and would like to pay at their perceived value. This means that they are, at the very minimum, interested in purchasing. This now becomes a closing strategy, which we will go over at the next stop.

Final check

This has been a long stop. We accomplished a lot here, so let's recap before we move on.

First, we shifted from the initial value building phase to the business side of the conversation. This transition should be smooth and nearly unrecognizable. With a rehearsed transition statement, you can effectively direct the conversation to business. Such possible transition statements are:

- "Let me make a recommendation to you."
- "Based on what you told me, I'd like to show you this."
- "I think you will appreciate what we have going on right now."

Once we transitioned, we can't go back. Now, we start with the *professional* and *product why*. We want to communicate to the prospect the reason for our brand to exist and what separates us from the rest. This should be one of the first things your prospect hears - it's all about positive association.

After we communicate the *why*, we start to talk about the product/service features. We describe the features that are important to the individualized prospect. We learned this information in the previous *Discovering a Need* stop, so there should be no need to guess. When we are talking about those features, we describe them in terms of their advantages (what makes the feature important/what it does) and their benefits (why it will benefit that prospect exclusively). This helps prospects associate value to your product/service.

Prospects will be skeptical by nature. Seeing is believing. They will want to see proof of our product/service demonstrating the value we just built up. This is where we can show them tangible evidence to back up our claims. Charts, graphs, statistics, and data are great ways we can show technical proof. We can also present intangible proof, which comes in the form of 3rd party stories. This also helps prospects because people naturally look to their peers for reassurance. Telling 3rd party stories gives us the chance to show the prospect that our product/service has actually worked for people in similar situations.

At this point, we have built up a lot of value in the eyes of the prospect. Now, we have to put a price on that value. By confidently stating our price while using positive language, we will show the prospect that we are confident in the price and in the value that it provides. We should never be apologetic about the price - confidence is the name of the game.

Here's our entire Safe Security pitch for the premium service, summed up to include all the points using only one FAB statement:

- "Mr. Jones, let me recommend this package to you because I feel it will fit your needs perfectly. Here is our premium package. One of the most important features we have in this package is our 24 hour monitoring service. We have a room of fully staffed and real associates ready to help at a moment's notice. If they notice any burglar activity or if the alarm is sounded, we will notify both you and the police at the same time. Police will get notified two times faster and will arrive at your house much quicker. You'll never have to worry about being on your own in an emergency - someone will always be there to help you regardless of the time or day and we will be there to help immediately. I have this graph that shows police response rates between us and the industry average, which includes our competition. As you can see, our response rate is half of the average. We measure our own times too - we have never had a response time that exceeded the average. On our worst day, we still beat the competition. A few months ago, my neighbor was out of town on business. His wife and child were home by themselves. Late at night, someone tried to gain entrance through a window with a crowbar. We caught it within seconds and the police were out there soon after. They were able to catch the suspect and nobody was hurt. My neighborhood is much safer now. This is by far our highest quality of service. It comes with all the important features that we discussed before plus a lifetime satisfaction guarantee. Your investment would only be $50/month for the best security services in town.

You will never feel unsafe or alone in an emergency again."

Now we are finally ready to move on and close the prospect!

Stop 5: The Close

"Everything you've ever wanted is on the other side of fear." - George Addair, 19th century entrepreneur and real-estate developer

---

This stop can be the most exciting and thrilling stop in the entire road trip. If you can successfully navigate this stop, you have the unique ability to shorten the road trip significantly by closing the sale right here. Although this is a difficult feat to accomplish, it's not at all impossible. If you have done all the proper work at the previous stops, and if you execute at this stop, you have a very strong possibility of earning some business.

Had this been a real road trip, this would be the last thirty minutes of traveling when we are nearly at our destination. Everyone is eager to arrive and excited to get to the part of your trip that you came for. This is the first true point in the conversation where the prospect will either agree or refuse to buy. It's the most anticipated part of your sales presentation. That's why previous to this, skipping stops is a bad idea. All the previous stops are designed to build on one another, all leading up to this point, where you will ask for the sale.

While asking for the sale might sound simple in theory, it actually involves a fair amount of psychology and science. Simply asking the prospect "So, do you want to buy it?" could be considered a closing statement (it's called the *Direct Close*), but it's probably not the most effective method you can use. There are many different closing methods and theories that people swear by. Most of them are tried and true strategies for getting the prospect to say "yes" that are rooted in both logic and psychology. Using these methods, you can greatly increase your chance of closing a sale at this stop and finishing your trip faster.

It should be noted that this stop, much like the previous stop, should have a smooth transition as well. Rather than placing a transition statement in here, this road map was designed for the pitch to naturally become the close. The best method of entering this stop is to have a closing strategy and statement ready immediately after you present the price. If you do a quick search online for "closing techniques," you'll find dozens upon dozens of different closing methods and strategies, each one wildly different from the previous. While there exists many different ways to close a prospect, we'll only focus on a select few that I have used with great success. In this stop, we'll go over the most effective, powerful, and simple options that you can use either in a face-to-face setting or over the phone.

Be firm

Before we jump right to the closing strategy itself, there are a few things that we have to consider first. At this point in our road trip, you should now realize that sales is a mixture of *what you say* and *how you say it*. In every stop, we have crafted our verbiage and our manner of speaking to correspond with our goal of the stop. The close is no different - we have to adjust our words and attitude accordingly.

Expect a "yes"

When closing a prospect, you are asking for their business. There is no doubt about that - at this point, the prospect is seemingly entirely in control of the conversation. For many sales professionals, this is the most vulnerable part of the process, so the natural reaction is to get defensive before we even close. It's no secret that salespeople have to be thick-skinned. Most of the time, the prospect will tell you "no." During my first professional sales job it was normal that most people (8/10 people) I would talk to would tell me "no." That knowledge was always in the back of my head. I would focus on the eight that would say "no" and not the two that would say "yes." By focusing on the possibly negative outcome, I would automatically get defensive during the close. Sometimes, my body language was even submissive. It's not that I was scared to hear "no," but rather, was preliminarily expecting the "no" before the prospect even said it. This prevented me from presenting a strong and assertive close. This hamstrung my process and definitely contributed to my initial lack of success.

Before we even start our first day of selling, we are told that most people will tell you "no." It's an unfortunate part of the job; no matter how good you are there will always be someone who simply will not buy, no matter how skilled you are. Even with that knowledge, the top performing salesperson will continue to break records and close more and more people. This is because the top performer has learned to change their mental attitude from *anticipating a no* to *expecting a yes*.

Back before we left for our road trip we 'checked our attitude' by focusing on our own emotional intelligence and taking advantage of our mental toughness. By doing that, we were able to start the call with a positive and productive attitude. The same basic principles apply here. It doesn't matter if you are expecting a prospect to say either "yes" or "no." At the end of the day, it's your decision and it's based on your attitude. If you are confident in the product/service, confident in the price, and confident that this product/service will benefit the prospect, you should be expecting a yes! It should be the case where if the prospect denies your pitch, you should be thinking "Wait, what? You DON'T want to buy? I don't understand."

Simply by expecting the prospect to say "yes," the close is going to sound more natural and more genuine. When you are confident in yourself and in the desired end result, the close is going to sound less forced, which means that you will sound more trustworthy. Remember, trust is one of the key elements for a successful road trip. This is a subtle, yet effective, way to add another layer of trust during one of the most pivotal parts of the trip.

Use powerful language

A lot of people will tell you that it's not what you say, but rather, how you say it. To some extent, this is true. However, for the purpose of this section (and the entire road trip), I would make the argument that selling is both what you say *and* how you say it. Your verbiage has to be clear and concise, yet the way you say your words has to make an impact on the prospect.

One of the top salespeople that I have ever met told me that the secret to his success was to use powerful language during the close. It sounds easier than it is. Closing a prospect can be one of the most intense parts of the road trip. It takes courage to go toe-to-toe with a prospect and ask for the sale. Things can get awkward really fast, which is why it can be easy to back down right away and ask for the sale in a weak and almost apologetic way. Top performing sales executives have learned to fight this urge and close using powerful language and terminology.

When we talk about using powerful language, we don't mean using demanding or threatening language. As always, we should be respecting the prospect and not forcing them to buy from us. At the end of the day, the prospect should know that we are only asking for them to purchase. We are not coercing them to do anything. All we want to do here is use terminology and language that shows the prospect that we truly believe that our product is perfect for them, and that they should in turn purchase it.

The best way you can improve your language at this part would be to first remove all weak verbiage from your vocabulary. Weak verbiage can be anything that might indicate that you are not that confident or sure of yourself:

- I think
- Maybe
- Possibly
- Might

Again, this probably looks easy on the surface. I thought the same thing too, until I looked at my own pitch at the time. Without even knowing it, my close started off with the same set of words. Every single time I would go and attempt to close a prospect, I would start out with "So, I think this will be a good fit for you, would you maybe…" then proceed with the actual close itself. After taking a look at my verbiage, I changed it to "I know this will be perfect for you. Let's do this…"

The change was subtle, but it changed my entire message. Previously, I was communicating to the prospect that I was really unsure about everything I just said. It was definitely subtle, but it was there. With the updated version, my message became one of confidence, belief, and trust.

Instead of using the previous words, try using the following:

- I know
- Definitely
- Without a doubt
- Absolutely

Be assumptive

Remember what we talked about before, where we should shift our attitude from expecting a "no" to a "yes?" The idea behind that was to be so sure of our product/service, that there was no possible way the prospect could say no. That can manifest itself in the verbiage right here.

Let's go back to my earlier example, where I would start my close with "So, I think this will be a good fit for you, would you maybe…" Notice the very last part. Rather than assuming that the prospect would buy, I said "would you maybe." This showed the prospect that I was not confident that they would say "yes," and even came off as being somewhat desperate. This is not at all what you want to be communicating to the prospect.

After changing the start of the closing statement, it became "I know this will be perfect for you. Let's do this…" Again, take note of the last part. Rather than being unsure of the prospect's answer, I assumed that they were going to say "yes," so my closing opener became assumptive rather than questioning. This seemingly subtle and miniscule change in words dramatically increased my closing rate. When I asked the top performing salesperson from before what his closing sounded like, he had the exact same line - "let's do this."

If we take the lessons here and apply it to our closing statement for the security system, it would sound the exact same. If we were selling boats instead, it would sound the same. The best thing about these closing statements is that they are practically universal for any product, any service, or any industry. Assumptive, powerful language will work, regardless of what you are selling.

Once we shift our attitude to focus on the positive and rework our language, we are finally ready to start the actual closing process, starting with building the urgency of the product/service.

Create urgency

Have you ever bought something 'on a whim' because the price was discounted for a limited time? How about because there was a limited quantity and they were selling fast? If so, whether you want to admit it or not, you bought because you felt the urgency to buy it while you have the chance. It could have been anything: clever discounting by the pricing team, a limited time offering, or a 'going out of business' sale. Regardless of the situation, someone or something created urgency for you to buy it right then.

Urgency is a powerful sales tool that should be an essential part of your closing strategy. It's a difficult thing to actually master – you have to put enough pressure on the prospect to buy, but not too much pressure to scare them away. If done correctly, you will have preliminarily overcome the common excuse of "I'll have to think about it and get back to you." This is a great way to put yourself in a favorable position of leverage with the prospect, so it helps you regain some of the power that the prospect currently has.

Make it scarce

One of the key components to being urgent is the mutual understanding that this is a scarce product/service and won't be around forever. Imagine this scenario: You are in the market for a new car and it's the end of the year. You're flipping through the newspaper when an advertisement falls out on the table. When you take a closer look at it, you see that the local car dealership is selling off all of this year's models off the lot as fast as possible to make way for the newer model. Once they are gone, they will not be selling them anymore. Being that you are in the market for a new car and you have heard good things about that model, you decide to check them out before they are all gone. The fact that there is a limited quality of the older models caused you to seriously consider that car for a possible purchase.

Our realtor did a great job with this when she was showing us the house with the eco-windows. We live in a pretty rapidly-growing area with a big military presence, where houses get sold or rented out pretty quickly. She told us that the house was on the market for over a couple months and the owners were looking at renting it out if they can't sell it soon. She told me they had some possible tenants who wanted to look at it that next day. This urgency was one of the reasons why we decided to place an offer on the house that day.

Scarcity does not always mean a limited product supply either. You could also make the price scarce by setting a limit on a discounted rate. If that dealership was selling the 2017 models this weekend only at a reduced rate, they are making the discounted price scarce. After this weekend, it will be priced at a normal rate. This might cause you to shorten your decision making process and buy that car today while it's reasonably priced.

The main idea behind making your product/service scarce is to set a limit on the product quantity, the time it's offered, or the time it's at a discounted price. If you can do this, the prospect will feel the need to make a decision right there, rather than thinking about it.

Let's say that we just pitched the prospect our premium security package, which was $50/month. Let's also say that this price is not the full price - it's been discounted for those people who sign up in August only. After August ends, the price returns to $75/month. This would be a great way to create some urgency for the prospect to make the decision today because that $50/month price is limited to this month only, making it scarce:

- "I know this will be perfect for you. Let's do this. The $50/month price is the discounted, locked-in rate for those who sign up this month. After the month ends, this same package returns to $75/month."

Confidently and assertively, we simply told the prospect a fact. The understanding that the price is only $50/month for a limited time should trigger something in the mind of the prospect that they need to make a decision here soon while they still have the chance.

Incorporate F.O.M.O. (Fear of Missing Out)

F.O.M.O (Fear of Missing Out) is a method that should be used in conjunction with scarcity. If the prospect does not want to make a decision right now, that's fine, but they will be missing out on something fantastic once the offer is over. If they miss out on the opportunity to purchase right now, they will have remorse later on for not taking advantage while the offer was so good. You have to be careful here though. You don't want to threaten the prospect or give anything that might be construed as an ultimatum. The strong-armed urgency pitches might work in the short term, but they are not conducive to long-term, sustained sales success. You can use the F.O.M.O. method in a low key manner by taking advantage of the 'Keeping up with the Joneses' sociological pattern and reiterating the consequence of waiting in a factual manner.

Keeping up with the Joneses

If your product/service is really popular and desirable, everyone who is purchasing is getting a valuable benefit to them. It has to be popular for a reason. If you tell your prospect that your product/service is extremely popular (and have the proof ready as well – don't lie!), they will realize that if everyone else is buying it, it has to be good. This goes hand-in-hand with the 3rd party stories from the previous stop. Remember, people automatically look to their peers for advice and purchasing reinforcement (that's why user review websites and apps are so popular). This is a way you can bring in that peer reinforcement to make your close much stronger.

This should flow naturally from your urgency statement. Not only will it only add to the overall urgency, but it will invoke feelings in the prospect of "if everyone else is buying this, they must be getting a benefit that I am not currently getting. I should have that as well." If you have ever heard of the term 'keeping up with the Joneses,' this is where that feeling is found. People don't want to be left behind from their peers or feel like everyone else has something that they do not have. According to the 'Keeping up with the Joneses' sociological pattern, not only do people look towards others for advice, they look at others to benchmark themselves against. If other people have goods or services that they themselves do not presently have, feelings of inferiority and jealousy will cause them to acquire those same goods or services.

While your goal should not be to make the prospect mad and jealous of others, by simply bringing up the fact that your product/service is popular should be a testament to the value and benefits that you presented. It will only strengthen the argument that this is a perfect product/service for them, as portrayed here:

- "I know this will be perfect for you. Let's do this. The $50/month price is the discounted, locked-in rate for those who sign up this month. After the month ends, this same package returns to $75/month. **So far, most of the families in this area have chosen this option**."

Reiterating the consequences of waiting in a factual manner

At this point your prospect should understand what the value and the benefits are for your product/service from the work you did during the previous stop. Let's reiterate how important it is: it's absolutely necessary for the prospect to understand how the product/service will benefit them individually. Once they understand, they will see the value. Once they do, the knowledge that the product/service/price might not be available soon might cause them to strongly consider a purchase. Again, this is why skipping stops is not advisable.

Perhaps this was a strong way to put it, but you should make sure the prospect understands the consequences for waiting to make a decision. This should not be done in a negative way (buy this now, or else!), but rather, in a gentle way. Our realtor told us that people could sign a lease agreement as early as tomorrow, so if we wait to make a decision, the house might not be available by the morning. It was a stern warning, but it gave us a real consequence if we waited too long.

This in itself is sometimes referred to as the 'Take-Away Close.' I would argue that this should not be used as your sole closing strategy, but merely as a technique used to build urgency leading up to the close itself.

Overall, creating urgency is an essential element of your sales pitch that should be included before the close. If you wait until after the close to bring urgency in, it will be much less genuine and much less effective. For example:

> *You:* "So, would you like to go ahead and go secure your house with this package?"
> *Prospect:* "Maybe, let me think about it and give you a call later on."
> *You:* "Well wait; hold on, this has been really popular around your area. For this month only, it is $50, and then returns to $75…"

At that point, your urgency statement will feel forced and might even feel untrue. If the prospect feels as if they are being lied to, your road trip will come to a sudden halt. This brings us to our next point about urgency: don't lie.

We have already gone over this topic, but it's so important that it's worth talking about again right here. It's crucial that you are ethical in your urgency statements. This portion of the sales presentation is the easiest part to lose your morals. Falsification of urgency is the same thing as lying. It not only erodes your prospect's trust in you, but has the possibility of ruining your reputation. Remember, the goal here is to not only close a sale, but to establish long-term sustained success. If you close a deal with dishonest and deceitful urgency statements, you have a strong chance of either losing a repeat customer, or having that sale rescind. Either way, you will be negatively impacted in the long run, so it's best to avoid all that and just stick with honest and truthful statements.

For those of you who have to sell a product right now, creating urgency is how you are able to close a prospect on the spot. When the sales cycle and the decision making process are very short, creating urgency allows for you to help the prospect to reach a favorable decision faster.

Close with a strategy

You cannot rely solely on the urgency to close the sale. While people might feel the pressure to buy because it's urgent, only a few will buy because of that. A great majority of people will not buy solely on the urgency alone. To become a top performing sales executive, you have to have a strategy and a method that you will use to actually ask for the business. Remember, it's both what you say and how you say it. The idea here is to use certain words, phrases, and sentences that guide the prospect to purchase.

No, this is not about deceiving the prospect in any way. If the product was truly not a good for the prospect, we should not even be this far in the road trip. No, I'm not on some moral high ground here - willingly leading a prospect to purchase something that is a bad fit or a bad decision for them will cause them to reconsider their purchase. Remember, we want loyal and happy customers, not ones that are disgruntled and upset. If you are at this point in the road trip, you should be confident that your product/service will solve a real problem. It's about helping the prospect realize that by buying and using it.

By having a closing strategy, you will immensely improve your chances of the prospect saying "yes." They can be difficult to master, but if used correctly, a proper closing strategy that is well-executed will separate you from the rest in terms of performance. Fortunately, there are literally dozens upon dozens of closing strategies that you can use. A simple internet search will yield all kinds of closing strategies, ranging from the *Balance Sheet Close* (making a pros and cons list for the prospect) to the *Yes-Set Close* (asking only "yes" questions so the prospect is more inclined to say "yes" to you). There are so many different ways that you can close a prospect that you could fill an entire book on this subject alone.

When I was researching the best ways to close, it was difficult to distinguish which methods would work and which ones were less effective. After many trial-and-error closes, I ended up being comfortable with only three main closing strategies. These three strategies are simple to learn, easy to master, and can be used in almost any situation, regardless of what you are selling. Again, these are my three personal favorite strategies - there are many more that exist out there, but these three resulted in more successful closes than the rest.

One thing that you will notice about the closing strategies presented here is that they are all somewhat assumptive by nature. Remember before when we talked about expecting a "yes" from the prospect? This is where that idea really manifests itself. All these closes essentially assume that the prospect is ready to purchase from you. Again, having the confidence to assume this is a powerful idea that can translate to more successful closes.

Alternative Close

The *Alternative Close* (also known as simply the *Choice Close*) is a technique that works by offering the prospect only two choices of your product/service. The idea here is that by offering the prospect two different alternatives, they will be more inclined to say "yes" to one of the options, rather than saying "no" to both of them. If you just ask the prospect if they want to buy something, the choices are either "yes" or "no." If you ask the prospect which option they want, the choice shifts to "offer A" or "offer B".

Recently, I was out to eat with my wife. We had just finished up the meal when our waiter came over and asked if we had any room for dessert. Usually, we say "no" to that question, even if the dessert menu looks good. However, this time, our waiter came over and said "I notice that you were eyeing the dessert menu - our two most popular choices are the cheesecake and the brownie. Which one should I bring for you?" We chose the cheesecake.

Notice that the waiter did not ask if we wanted dessert. He assumed that we were going to order, so he presented the two best choices and asked which one we wanted. While this was a relatively minor purchasing decision, his wording was enough for us to break the habit of saying "no" to dessert because not having dessert was not presented to us as an option.

Also, notice that the waiter gave us only two choices. He did not give us three, four, or five different choices. The *Alternative Close* should be limited to two choices. Any more than that, and the prospect might get overwhelmed and confused. While you might believe that giving the prospect more choices means that they will surely find one option that works for them, many prospects will have a hard time focusing on the individual options and will only focus on the huge number of options. For example, if our waiter gave us seven different dessert options to choose from, I probably would have told him that dessert won't be necessary - not because I didn't want dessert, but because there were too many options to choose from right there in that moment. Some people will argue that three choices should be presented. I agree that for a close, three choices are acceptable, but three choices actually fall into a different closing strategy, which we will talk more about later.

This close works because the prospect feels as if they are making a choice based on their own free will. If the prospect feels like they are in control and are choosing what option is best for them, they have a much higher chance of picking one rather than declining both. That being said, you should not be presenting two options to the prospect that don't make sense for them. If you are going to present two choices to the prospect, both options have to ultimately be beneficial to them. Ideally, one should be slightly more attractive than the other. The more attractive offer should be the one that you were building the value for, while the other option should be there as a simple alternative to "no." In either instance, whichever the prospect chooses, they should be able to have a great experience with the product/service and it should still solve the need that we previously uncovered.

When it comes to closing our prospect on our security services, we can easily employ the *Alternative Close* by offering two similar packages with different price points:

- "I know this will be perfect for you. Let's do this. The Premium Package $50/month price is the discounted, locked-in rate for those who sign up this month. After the month ends, this same package returns to $75/month. So far, most of the families in this area have chosen this option. **However, we also have a package that has most of the same benefits as the Premium Package without the mobile app or the instant accessibility to your house. This package is normally $25/month, but our rate for this month is $20/month. Which option would you prefer?**"

Even though we presented two options, we still took advantage of the previous principles of assumption, making the product/service scarce, and employed the fear of missing out.

Notice the last sentence of the close: "Which option do you prefer?" That's where the idea of you expecting a "yes" comes into play. Now, the choice is between offer A and offer B. If we had asked the prospect "Would you like to choose one of these?" the choice now becomes "yes" or "no." By phrasing your close in a way where the prospect has to choose one product or the other, you can greatly increase your chances of the prospect purchasing while giving the prospect the idea of free will and free choice. In this sense, this is one of my favorite closing techniques and I use this one most often.

Assumptive Close

One of the underlying principles of the closing section is to expect a "yes." This close takes that idea and significantly amplifies it. Whereas the previous *Alternative Close* gave the prospect a choice between two different options (we assumed the prospect would at least choose one of the two options), the *Assumptive Close* basically works by assuming that the prospect already agreed to buy your product/service.

This is one of the most common closes used. It's popular because by assuming that the prospect has already agreed to buy, you are essentially showing that you are so confident in your product that saying "no" would be the most unwise and surprising decision ever. When the prospect hears an *Assumptive Close*, the idea is that they will agree that this works for them and will proceed with the purchase.

This close works by jumping to the next level immediately, such as delivery details, installation specifics, payment options, etc. Much like the previous close, this should not end with a question of "So, you want to buy it, right?" Although that is indeed assumptive, it's still presenting the prospect with a clear "yes" or "no" decision.

An effective *Assumptive Close* will look something like this:

- "I know this will be perfect for you. Let's do this. The Premium Package $50/month price is the discounted, locked-in rate for those who sign up this month. After the month ends, this same package returns to $75/month. So far, most of the families in this area have chosen this option. **When would you like for us to install this system?**"

We did not ask if the prospect wanted us to install the system because ultimately that's a choice between "yes" and "no." This question assumes that the prospect has essentially already bought our services. Now, it's just a question of installation details. The best part about this close is that it's a natural transition to the next stop, which is the part where we lock in the sale. If the prospect ultimately answers you with an affirmative statement, you are clear to proceed directly to the next stop.

Bracket Close

Remember when we talked about the *Alternative Close* and how we should only present two choices? In some instances, presenting three choices can be equally as effective (if not more so) if done correctly. The *Bracket Close* is the method that you should use if presenting three purchasing options. It works by first presenting the prospect with an expensive option that might be above their budget. Next, you present an option that is within their budget (ideally, this is the option that you are trying to sell to them). Last, you present an option that is far less expensive than the first option, but only a little less expensive than the middle option.

This close works for a variety of reasons. The first reason is that when the prospect first hears the expensive option, that's their new benchmark. If you present the low-cost option first, they will be focusing on that and will ignore all the other options. If the prospect compares everything to the high cost option first, they will have a stronger propensity to choose a lower cost option. By presenting the lowest cost option last, they will see that one as being the least beneficial to them because it costs so little in comparison. If the price is somewhat close to the middle one, the prospect should be thinking "For only X amount of dollars more, I can get all this..." After their analysis, they should choose the middle option, which is the one you are aiming for.

In other words, the prospect rejecting the highest cost option gives the prospect the feeling of saving money, while rejecting the lowest cost option gives the prospect the feeling of buying a good quality product. This is very similar to the *Alternative Choice* close because you are giving the prospect the idea of free choice between three options that you presented. "No" is not an option that was presented, so the probability that they will choose one of the three is high. Even if the prospect chooses the lowest cost option, it's still far better than the prospect not buying anything at all.

You may have seen this close happen in real life. It's a common close to use in retail stores and online shopping websites. A while back, I was shopping around online for a new laptop. I knew that I wanted a laptop that was tailored mostly for blogging and writing. The website I was looking at presented me with three different options of the same laptop. The first option was loaded with memory, had the best processor and graphics card available, and had a large screen. This option, of course, was very expensive. The next option had what I would call 'standard' features - a good processor, a good amount of memory, a standard graphics card, etc. This option was much less expensive. The last option was stripped of all the bells & whistles, had a really small screen, and was FAR less expensive than the most expensive one, but marginally less expensive than the middle one. I chose the middle one. Unknowingly, I was closed using the bracket method without anyone actually selling to me. If a website can effectively use this, just imagine what you can do as a professional salesperson.

For our security system close, we have to adjust our structure a little bit to account for all three options:

- **"I have three recommendations that I know will be great for you. The Platinum Package is listed for $100/month - it includes everything you were looking for, coverage for every single one of your windows and doors, and free system upgrades for life. The Premium Package also has everything you were looking for.** $50/month price is the discounted, locked-in rate for those who sign up this month. After the month ends, this same package returns to $75/month. So far, most of the families in this area have chosen this option. **If you are on a very tight budget, I also have the Silver Package, which has your basic monitoring and response services without the mobile app/instant accessibility. This option is $25/month. Which option would you prefer?"**

Clearly, this is very similar to the *Alternative Choice* close. The last sentence is the exact same and the same psychological principles apply here. The only difference is that you are offering three strategic choices that are designed to motivate the prospect to pick the middle one. This close is great because it's a win-win-win. If the prospect chooses the most expensive option, great! If they choose the middle option, great! If they choose the least expensive option, it's still a sale, which is great! In either scenario, you can move along to the next stop.

Don't say a word

Before you drive straight to the next stop after the close, there is one more thing that you have to do. I'm sure that at some point, you have heard the expression "The one who talks first loses." This is what that expression is referring to. After the closing statement, you should remain absolutely silent and wait for the prospect to respond.

This is possibly one of the most weird components of the entire road trip. It's weird because it's incredibly easy to comprehend and understand, yet incredible difficult to actually do. It's incredibly difficult because people hate awkwardness. Salespeople are no different. When nobody is talking, things can get very awkward extremely quickly. You might feel the pressure or the urge to say *something* just to break the silence, but you should do all you can to fight the feelings. The prospect is feeling the same exact pressure to talk as well. The difference is, the prospect is feeling the pressure to make a decision. If you start to talk past the close, it delays the decision making process for the prospect. If you continue to talk past the close, you are metaphorically spinning your wheels and not going anywhere.

It doesn't really matter if the prospect sits there for one minute or ten minutes. Sit there in silence and wait for the prospect to respond. Luckily, most prospects only take a few seconds to think about it, but those fifteen to thirty seconds can feel like an eternity. This is the one part of the road trip where you are allowed to tune out for a moment and think about something else. Know that the prospect is taking these moments to weigh their options and make a decision - all you have to do is sit there and wait. Again, this is easy to understand, but difficult to actually do.

If you are successful here, the prospect will come back with an answer. They can't sit there forever. In a perfect situation, the prospect will answer in the affirmative and the sales process can proceed. If they come back with a "no," we can handle that road block easier than you might think.

Final check

The close is one of the most intense places that we will stop. This is the place where sales are made. If we skip this stop, the possibility of us reaching our final destination is slim to none. It takes a lot of courage to ask the prospect for the sale. Luckily, we have ways and strategies that allow for us to do so in a confident manner using psychological methods that increase our chance for success.

First, we adjusted our overall attitude by expecting a "yes" rather than a "no." This dramatically helps our confidence when we actually go for the close. By using powerful language, such as "definitely" and "absolutely," we communicate that we are not only sure of ourselves, but sure of the product/service. We are also being assumptive by assuming that this product/service is perfect for them and that there is absolutely no reason why they would not want to purchase it.

We created urgency for the prospect by making it scarce and incorporating the fear of missing out (F.O.M.O.). This removes the common excuse of "I have to think about it" from the prospect. It not only motivates them to make a decision right here and now, but also motivates them to agree to a purchase.

Finally, we closed using a specific strategy. We either went with the *Alternative Choice* close, the *Assumptive*

Close, or the *Bracket Close*. The actual close that you use can be one of dozens that exist out there. The only thing that matters is that we closed using a specific strategy that is designed to help the prospect answer in the affirmative.

After the close, we stop talking and we wait for the prospect to answer. At this point, our trip can go one of two ways. If the prospect answers "yes" or answers in the affirmative, we can now proceed to our final destination, which is the stop where we officially lock in the sale! If the prospect decides not to purchase, we have a significant road block in front of us that we have to get through before we can move on to the next stop. If the prospect tells us "no," we have to figure out why they don't want to buy and overcome those objections.

Road Block: Objections

"Obstacles do not block the path; they are the path." - Zen Proverb

---

We have done a lot of work so far. We gained the trust of the prospect, we uncovered a true problem or need that the prospect is experiencing, and we pitched a product/service that solves that particular problem or need. We have accomplished so much in the way of persuasion that it seems almost inconceivable that someone would ever say "no" to us. After all, if our product/service is a perfect fit for them individually, how could they refuse?

The unfortunate reality is that many prospects will refuse your first proposal. Human beings, it seems, are wired to say "no" to people, even those who can help them out. I'm sure that you have done this without even thinking of it: imagine a scenario where you are in a shopping mall and walk into a shoe store. You are not sure which exact shoe you want, but know that you are looking for running shoes. When you walk inside the store, you are greeted by a shoe salesperson who asks "May I help you with anything?" Even though you came in the store for running shoes in particular, your first automatic response is "No thank you, just browsing."

Sound familiar? Perhaps you might have done this before. I can tell you with confidence that I certainly have. It's not that I dislike the shoe salesperson and it's not that I distrust them either; saying "no" is just a common knee-jerk response. If you combine that with the fact that some people have legitimate reservations about buying, you can easily see how common it is to hear "no." To say that you will close 100% of the prospects that you talk to without handling some objections is absurd. It doesn't matter how good you are. At some point, you <u>will</u> hit this extremely common road block and have to decide if you want to overcome it and be successful or give up, turn back, and head home.

The funny thing is that our road trip, in all actuality, is almost over. The finish line is within reach, yet so many times salespeople give up at the first sight of objections because they have the unfortunate misconception of being the most difficult obstacles that you will have to overcome. Oftentimes, when salespeople hear an objection, they lose all momentum that they have gained so far. They believe that the prospect really hates the product/service, which causes them to quit even if the final destination is right ahead. The truth is, objections can be handled in many instances with a simple method that is very effective.

<u>Know your common objections and prevent them from happening</u>

There is a quote that comes from 20th century philosopher Alfred A. Montapert that accurately summarizes how to overcome customer objections and problems: "Expect problems and eat them for breakfast." While he was not directly talking about handling objections during the sales process, the meaning behind the quote fits perfectly. The idea is that in life, there will certainly be problems. Regardless of who you are, one day, something is going to go wrong eventually. To help you overcome problems as they arise, you should know what the potential problems are and know how to overcome them ahead of time.

This is not a new or a radical idea. Thousands of years before that, legendary Chinese general and military strategist Sun Tzu wrote a book called *The Art of War.* The book focuses on military tactics and strategy for a victory in warfare. The book has been highly influential and has become a beacon of ancient intelligence. Even today, it remains an important work that influences modern military leaders. Little of the book is actually about engaging in actual military battles - it mostly focuses on outsmarting the enemy. Because of that, it also has influenced business professionals, lawyers, educators, professional football coaches, and many others. One of the lessons in the book is about knowing your enemy. The quote directly states: "Know your enemy and know yourself and you can fight a thousand battles without disaster."[4] By knowing your enemy, you will have an easier time working out a strategy that plays to their weaknesses using your own strong points. Again, the same idea applies here: know your objections and use a strategy that plays to the weak part of the objection.

Another takeaway is that you should take measures to prevent disasters from happening in the first place. If you know what your objections are going to be ahead of time, you can take the necessary steps to prevent them from taking place. This is comparable to those gasoline additives bought at gas stations and auto stores that clean your injection system. If you know that one day, your injection system might get dirty or clogged; why not use a cleaner to prevent it from happening? Same idea applies here. If you know your objections, work on overcoming them early on.

At this point, you might be feeling slightly overwhelmed. Depending on the industry that you work in, there may be potentially dozens of different objections that you could be working with - perhaps even hundreds.

Looking at objections from many different industries and companies, patterns emerge. While there may be many different variations and flavors of objections, there seems to be only a handful of basic ones that pop up more often than the others. These core objections encompass many smaller objections too. For example, if someone tells you that your price is too expensive and someone else tells you that they are happy with their current provider who is less expensive, the core objection between the two is the prospect does not see the value. If you memorize these individual styles of objections, you can handle any of them that come your way.

Lack of need objections

The first style of objection is an apparent lack of need for the product/service. This manifests itself in statements such as "I really don't think that option is for us," "I'm having a hard time seeing how this benefits us," "Things are going just fine right now, I'm happy with my current situation," or even the direct "I just don't think I need it."

Ideally you should not hear this objection style very often in the first place if you followed the steps correctly. One of the major guiding principles of this road map is to uncover and sell to help a real need. That's the ultimate purpose of the *Discovering a Need* stop - to remove these style of objections from the mind of the prospect at the very beginning. While this can be difficult to do, it ultimately ends with an ethical sale and a happy customer who is less prone to rescind on the sale.

However, even if you uncover a real need and respond to that need, prospects might still present a need objection. If this happens, it's a pretty good indication that the prospect might have another hidden need that was not revealed to us earlier. It might be the case that the prospect was not even aware of the need themselves at the time. It's also a good indication that the value of the benefits may not have been fully absorbed by the prospect. If a prospect has either a different actual need or they don't see the benefits of your product/service, they will have a legitimate lack of need objection.

The best offense is a good defense. This is why it's important to know your objection possibilities ahead of time. You can spend more time on the *Discovering a Need* stop to keep uncovering needs if you want to. You can clarify with the prospect that the need is legitimate. You can over-communicate the benefits. All these simple activities act as preventative maintenance on the road trip - they help remove the possibility of this road block.

If someone gives you this objection though, the best thing that you can do is to apologize for the misunderstanding and try to reconfirm what their real need is. If you were correct with their need, you know that you have to do a better job explaining the features, advantages, and benefits to them in a way that works for them individually. If you were originally incorrect on their need, the best that we can do is essentially go back to revisit the *Discovering a Need* stop.

We will review the actual strategy later on in this road block, but for now, just remember that when someone hits you with a need-objection, either re-explain the benefits of your product/service or head back to stop 3 and rediscover the real need.

Price objections

The second objection style comes in the form of price objections. Anything that falls in the category of price, cost, or money can be treated as a general objection to the price of the product/service. If a prospect feels that it costs too much/too little, they have a fundamental objection to the price. If someone tells you they simply cannot afford your product, it's ultimately an objection to the price. Overall, these price objections are some of the most common that you'll receive.

A lot of prospects use the price objection because it's one of the easiest things to protest. At the end of the day, we humans are private about our financial situations. I'm sure we have all thought "If I say the price is too much, who are you to tell me what I can and can't afford? You don't know my individual situation." The same rationale is being used by prospects that use price as an objection.

If you really think about it, although the objection is about the price, in reality, it's not. Remember, the price of the product/service that you sell is only as good as the value that you built up with the features, advantages, and benefits. If you fail to provide enough benefits for the prospect to satisfy them, the price won't be worth it. I know a guy who bought a new car for $55,000 cash but refused to pay $10 for a six pack of beer. His objection? "Too expensive for what it is." Obviously, the real objection wasn't that the beer was too expensive, but that the beer did not provide him with enough benefits to justify spending $10.

The same logic applies here. In many cases, a price objection is a misunderstanding disguised as an objection. Preventative maintenance for this style includes spending more time on the F.A.B. section and the price section in stop 4. The more relevant features, advantages, and benefits that you describe, the higher the value/worth should be in the mind of the prospect. Also, make sure you give special attention to the benefits portion. The prospect should understand why the features are beneficial to them individually. Doing this is probably the best way you can prevent price objections from happening.

As mentioned before, price objections are indeed some of the most common that you'll receive. While doing the above can certainly help prevent price objections, many prospects will almost automatically object to the price because it's easy. As uncomfortable as it is to talk about a disagreement in price, you're going to have to do it quite often if you want to close more sales and succeed. This is why it's important to rehearse strategies of how you will handle objections ahead of time.

We'll go over the actual strategy in the next section, but for now, know that if presented with a price objection, you'll want to resell the value and benefits of the product/service. If you are selling multiple tiered products (such as presenting three options), another strategy you could use will be to drop down to the lower cost option. Regardless, if rehearsed and done right you could easily overcome this objection style and be one stop closer to a closed sale.

Fear of change objections

Fear of change objections are also some of the most common that you'll receive. This objection style is interesting because this objection is rooted in a deep human trait that has been with us since the dawn of time. Despite the fact that humanity as a whole has grown so rapidly, explored so much, and accomplished so many things in a relatively short period of time, we humans seem to be resistant to change on an individual level.

Perhaps it's the trait that led us to form societies and civilizations, so we can abandon the ever changing life of the nomad. Within those societies and civilizations, people like for things to be constant. Predictability means that there are no sudden threats, so when massive change happens people have the instinct to panic. It doesn't matter if it's something as big as a governmental change in power or a promotion to a new job title. Change is tough to accept. Even for prospects that are making the decision to buy, that's still a change in their life. Again, you could be selling a multimillion dollar manufacturing contract to a large corporation or a security system to a single family - the idea of people are instinctively resistant to change still holds true.

These objections will go along the lines of "I think I'm still happy with my current situation" or "We already have success with our current situation, I feel no need to change it." Anything that points to the status quo as being acceptable is essentially an objection rooted in the desire to resist change. The way you can prevent these from happening is very similar to the lack of need objection. Make sure that you uncover the real need and pitch the product/service to fix that need specifically.

People don't like being told that what they are currently doing is wrong. If you come in and insist that your product/service is so much better than what they currently have, they might get defensive. When presented with an objection like this, you have to delicately tell them that your product solves a need that is currently being unmet by their current situation. You know that this need is being unmet because the prospect told you that it existed in the first place. Unless the prospect lied, there is a fundamental issue with their current situation that needs to be addressed. Reminding the prospect of the problem or need that they are experiencing will be our best way to overcome this objection style.

"Not right now" objections

Objections that indicate the prospect maybe wants to purchase (but not right at this moment) fall in this category. These objections always sound very similar to each other; "This sounds great, let me think about it and let you know!" or "Oh wow, that's good. I have to ask my wife about it and let you know later." Basically, any objection that is trying to delay a decision is a "not right now" objection.

Ideally, just like the lack of need objection, you should not hear this one very often if you take the proper preventative care steps. In many cases, when a prospect tells you that they might buy later on, it probably indicates that you did not build up enough urgency during the close stop. The best way to prevent this from happening is to simply never drive past the *Create Urgency* step. Every single time you take this road trip, never skip the urgency exit. If you do, there is a very high chance that this objection will pop up.

If you accidentally forget to create urgency (don't worry - it happens all the time, even to the best salespeople), don't panic. You can still overcome this objection pretty easily. The interesting thing about this objection is that it's either one of two things: a smokescreen excuse for a different objection (more likely) or a legitimate objection to the timing of the sale (less likely).

If it's a smokescreen excuse, you can seek to find the real objection using the strategy in the next section. If it's a real objection, you can still easily overcome it by incorporating the *Fear of Loss* strategy. Much like in the close when we used the *Fear of Missing Out*, the same idea applies here. You'll want to communicate the fact that waiting could result in the opportunity no longer being available. Removing the possibility of the prospect being able to solve their problems/needs will hopefully trigger an internal drive to act now.

Trust objections

The last style of objection that you'll hopefully never see is the trust objection. These objections are not rooted in a misconception of value or benefit, but rather, a fundamental distrust in you, your company, or your product/service. As we all know, trust is one of the cornerstones of a successful sales call. We spent the entire first two stops building enough trust to sustain us for the rest of the road trip. That's basically the entire idea of all the stops, to build a bridge of trust between you and the prospect. You won't see these objections very often because ideally, if the prospect told you their real need, they probably already trust you.

However, no matter how much trust you build with a prospect, you might still be seen as just another salesperson in their eyes. You are an outsider to their company and their lives trying to show them what's best. Because of this, there might be a lingering feeling of distrust from the prospect. Don't get offended. While you might want to take it personal, imagine yourself in their shoes. Whenever you go to purchase something, I'm sure you always bring a healthy amount of skepticism to the table. It's how we are able to distinguish deceiving advertisements from legitimate information. When a prospect is listening to your pitch, you better believe that they are 'sizing you up' with the same skeptical eyes. Because of that, while they are rare, you might occasionally find yourself staring at a trust objection.

Trust objections are easy to spot because the prospect will almost always tell you point blank "I'm sorry, but I really don't believe that this will work" and "I just don't trust that this is a good decision for me." You might also hear something more stinging too, like "I don't trust your company" or "I don't believe you." These are all obviously trust objections, and just like the previous, there are things we can do to prevent these from happening.

The best way you can avoid trust objections is by doing a few key things. First, don't move on in the road trip unless you have developed enough trust and rapport in stops one and two. If you go to discover a need without building trust, you might end up getting a fake need that is not real. In this case, you won't only be battling a need objection, but a trust one too. Second, make sure you are constantly confirming that the prospect understands your explanations during the pitch. Lastly, you should always be 100% genuine and authentic during the entire process. The prospect will know if you are actually trying to help them or not. Be genuine and you'll get the trust. I once had a sales mentor tell me "if you fail to build trust because you were not genuine, shame on you."

If, after all that, you do get a trust objection, they can still be overcome with the procedure in the next section. Ideally, you will want to go back to the "prove it" exit at the pitch stop. Proof of your product/service working remains one of the best ways that you can build trust with the prospect.

I E.A.T.

Now that we know our five objection types, we can move on to the actual strategy used to overcome them. The strategy works with any objection presented to you because it's designed to be a one-sized-fits-all procedure to handling objections. Earlier, we looked at the quote "Expect problems and eat them for breakfast." The procedure that we'll use is designed to help us 'eat' the objections with ease. Appropriately, it's called the *I E.A.T. Method of Objection Handling*.

Full disclosure: this is a goofy acronym that I created, but it is easy to remember and defines the steps in the strategy that we will use to overcome every objection that comes our way. No matter what the prospect says to us, we can use this strategy because it's designed to work with every objection style out there. It can also work outside of sales - I E.A.T. is a great strategy to use when there is a disagreement between two parties. If you and your friend disagree on a topic, you can use this strategy to get your point across.

The reason why this strategy works so well is that it allows for us to respond to the objection without the conversation becoming an argument. As we all know, arguments hardly solve anything. The only thing that an argument accomplishes is that it leaves both parties more upset and there is never really an agreement on a solution. If you begin to argue with the prospect, you might as well turn the car around and head back home right now, because the chance of reaching the final destination just became very slim.

To avoid this from happening, follow the steps in the *I E.A.T. Method of Handling Objections*:

> **I**dentify the problem
> **E**mpathize with the prospect
> **A**ffirmation of the problem
> **T**ackle the objection

Identify the problem

Let's say that the prospect simply tells you "no" after you try to close them. Rather than explain their objection to you right away, they just refuse to buy without a known reason. This doesn't happen very often. Usually prospects will give you their objection right after saying "no." If the prospect does state their objection to you first, you may skip this part and move to the next one - Empathize with the prospect.

In a few instances, the prospect will just say "no," followed by nothing. If this happens, the first thing that you are going to want to do is identify the problem. Without knowing what the objection is, there is no way we can possibly change the prospect's mind.

The best way to identify the problem is to simply ask the prospect themselves. This can feel a little awkward at first, especially for those who dislike confrontation. It takes a lot of courage to get the guts to ask the prospect why they refuse, especially if the prospect gives you a hard no at first. As awkward as it might feel, this is a crucial step to overcoming objections. If you don't do this, the strategy will not work, and you will not close a sale. It's as simple as that.

To identify the problem, one of the best things to do is act a little surprised at first. This subtle psychological move is meant to show the prospect that we're not used to hearing "no" because this product/service is so popular or works so well. If you act as if you agree with their objection, they will validate themselves without you even knowing it.

After the initial surprise, we have to then ask for clarity from the prospect. Don't just blurt out "But why?" as that can be interpreted as argumentative. The idea here is to have the prospect tell you what's wrong without them getting defensive over it. The best way we can do that is to respectfully ask, almost as if out of curiosity.

> ***Prospect:*** "No."
> ***You:*** "Oh, ok...not many people turn this offer down. May I ask, what's your hesitation?"

If you notice, we also told the prospect that "not many people turn this offer down." Again, just like in the previous sections, we want to invoke the *Fear of Missing Out* element here, along with the validation that the prospect knows that their peers are using it as well.

You can vary the wording as much as you deem fit, the main takeaway here is to have a go-to statement that you can use to identify an objection when someone tells you "no."

- "Hmm...alright. If you don't mind me asking, what is holding you back?"

If you ask a question like that, the prospect is forced to respond. After the statement, much like the close, don't say a word and wait for the prospect to respond. Again, this part can feel very awkward. The prospect feels the awkwardness too. This strategy is designed to work in those awkward parts of human interaction. Provided you don't fold under the awkwardness, the prospect should divulge information with ease. In this case, they should provide you with a basic objection.

For the purpose of the example, let's return to the security company pitch. Let's suppose that we attempted to close the prospect using an alternative close:

You: "I know this will be perfect for you. Let's do this. The Premium package $50/month price is the discounted, locked-in rate for those who sign up this month. After the month ends this same package returns to $75/month. So far, most of the families in this area have chosen this option. However, we also have a package that has the same benefits as the Premium package without the mobile app or instant accessibility. This package is normally $25/month, but our rate for this month is $20/month. Which option would you prefer?"

Prospect: "Uhm, no, I don't think I want either one."

You: "Oh...if you don't mind me asking, what's preventing you from trying us out?"

We then wait for the prospect to give us the objection. In the previous section, we went over the five basic styles of objections (no need, price, fear of change, not right now, and trust). In this section, we'll work with one objection for each style and work to overcome all the objection styles for the remainder of this stop.

- No need objection: "Well, I just don't think our family needs your security services."
- Price objection: "Honestly, that's out of our budget. Your prices are a little too high for me."
- Fear of change objection: "We are very happy with our current provider and do not want to leave them."
- Not right now objection: "That sounds like a good idea, but I have to talk it over with my wife."
- Trust objection: "I have a hard time believing that I'm going to get all this without some catch."

In any event, you have your objection, or at least something to work with. Even if it's not the real objection, you should still stick to the strategy - we will uncover the real objection later on if this one is not real. Regardless of what the prospect tells you, you can now move on to the next step in the strategy.

Empathize with the prospect

At this point, instinct might be to respond to the objection right away. You might have an urge to present your case as to why the prospect is mistaken in their objection. Many people accidentally do this without even realizing it. This results in nothing more than an argument, which as stated before, we want to avoid at all costs.

This is easier said than done. At this point, the prospect has stated a clear reason why they do not want to purchase. Even if it's a minor issue in your eyes, it could be a major one for them. In their head, they believe that this reason is so important that it is preventing them from buying right now. Naturally, their defenses will be up and they will be ready to defend their point of view. How then can we respond without starting a fight?

Rather than just retort back to the prospect, you should empathize with the prospect. Empathy is a powerful tool because it's rarely used during a disagreement. Most people are expecting you to argue with them, but simply by expressing empathy you almost catch them off guard.

You might be thinking that empathizing with a prospect's objection validates the objection for the prospect. If you are thinking that, you can be correct. This part of the strategy has to be done *just right* in order to be successful. There is a fine line that you must be mindful about. You want to empathize with the *feelings* of the prospect, not agree that their objection is justified.

We can do this by putting ourselves in the shoes of the prospect and, as stated before, empathize with what they are feeling. This is where we can employ the famous *Feel-Felt-Found* technique.

Feel-Felt-Found

The idea is to put yourself in the mind of the prospect and see how they are feeling. However, you can try all you want, but unfortunately, you just cannot do that successfully. No matter what, you'll never know what a prospect is going through individually. It's no good to empathize by only saying "I know what you mean" or "I know what you're feeling" because you don't know. The prospect knows that you don't know and you'll come off as far less genuine.

Rather, the *Feel-Felt-Found* technique can be used by describing other people in similar situations and their experiences. It sounds more difficult than it actually is. You can honestly use the same *Feel-Felt-Found* statement for mostly all objections because it can apply to any situation. For example:

> ***Prospect:*** "Uhm, no, I don't think I want either one."
> ***You:*** "Oh...if you don't mind me asking, what's preventing you from trying us out?"
> ***Prospect:*** "Honestly, that's out of our budget. Your prices are a little too high for me"
> ***You:*** **"I understand what you are *feeling*. Many people *felt* the same way when they looked at our services, however, when they tried us out they *found* that the investment was well worth it."**

With a statement like that, you accomplish a couple different things. Firstly, you are showing the prospect that you are not going to argue or dispute their feelings. Their feelings are very real to them and they will certainly get aggressively defensive if you challenge them. By empathizing, you are showing them that it's ok to feel that way. However, you are also communicating that others felt the same way, but found that they made a wise decision. It's showing the prospect that you are confident in the product and will stand by the prices.

After you empathize with the *Feel-Felt-Found* technique, you can now move on to the next step: clarification of the problem behind the objection in a manner that you can respond to.

Affirmation of the problem

At this point, the only thing that we really have to work with is the original objection that the prospect gave us. In a sense, this is only a one-sided vantage point of the situation. Oftentimes, the objection is vague and nondescript. Even if someone confidently and directly says "I don't need it," that can still be considered vague. What exactly don't they need? Why do they feel as if they don't need it? These are all things to take into consideration when someone presents you with a basic objection. That's why you have to affirm what the problem is by repeating it back to the prospect.

By you repeating what the problem is, you will be able to gain agreeance with the prospect on what the issue is. If you and the prospect agree on the problem, you can overcome that problem directly. Not to mention, this is a crucial time in the road trip. A lot of salespeople call this part "going to battle" because of the argumentative potential here. If you are able to get the prospect to agree with you on anything, it will make overcoming the objection much easier.

You can't, however, agree on what the prospect originally told you. Remember, their objection is usually vague. We want to make their objection clearer. The more clear and well-defined their objection becomes the better chance you have of overcoming it. The way to do this is to reword their objection so that it is better suited to respond to.

You might be stressing out again because this implies that you'll have to memorize hundreds of objections and know how to reword them. Don't worry; remember there are only five basic objection types. If you are able to take any objection and classify it into one of those five styles, you'll only have to memorize five ways to reword objections.

In this sense, we have to change the original instructions of the step to: Affirm what the problem is by repeating it back to the prospect *in your own words*. When you do this, it's always a good idea to make it clear that you are trying to gain a deeper understanding only to help the prospect:

- "Alright, I just want to make sure we're on the same page here, you are hesitant to try us because…"

After that, we can proceed with affirming the objection in our own words with the prospect.

Objection Style	Objection
No need	"Well, I just don't think our family needs your security services."
Price	"Honestly, that's out of our budget. Your prices are a little too high for me."
Fear of change	"We are very happy with our current provider and do not want to leave them."
Not right now	"That sounds like a good idea, but I have to talk it over with my wife."
No trust	"I have a hard time believing that I'm going to get all this without some catch."

Let's reword each objection accordingly:

Objection Style	Reworded
No need	"You don't see how our services can benefit your family in a way that is important to you."
Price	"The product investment is too high for the benefit return you will receive."
Fear of change	"You feel as if your current provider is sufficiently meeting your needs."
Not right now	"You want to give us a try, but need to confirm your decision with your wife."
No trust	"You don't trust that our services can deliver what is being promised."

By strategically rewording the objection in a manner in which you can respond to, you suddenly are able to regain control of the conversation, which is absolutely crucial in this step. The way that you reword your objections will probably vary from the examples above. The overall point is to take the original objection and rephrase it in a manner that you can work with.

After you reword the objection, you have to gain agreement with the prospect regarding this being the correct objection. If the prospect agrees with what you said, you are clear to respond to it. The best way of doing this is to simply ask if that's all that's holding them back!

> ***Prospect:*** "Uhm, no, I don't think I want either one."
> ***You:*** "Oh...if you don't mind me asking, what's preventing you from trying us out?"
> ***Prospect:*** "We are very happy with our current provider and do not want to leave them."
> ***You:*** "I understand what you are feeling. Many people felt the same way when they looked at our services, however, when they tried us out, they found that the investment was well worth it. **But I just want to make sure we are on the same page here - the reason you are hesitant to try us out is that you feel as if your current provider is sufficiently meeting your needs. Is that all that's preventing you from trying us out?**"

By doing this, you are not only rewording the objection, but isolating it. If the prospect agrees that this is all that's holding them back, you can now move on to the next step and respond to the objection. If they deny that this is the only reason holding them back, don't panic. Just repeat the previous steps until you get the real objection. The prospect really has no clear reason to lie to you about an objection, so simply by following the process, you should uncover the real objection at some point.

Tackle the objection

Now that you figured out what the real objection is, you can proceed to actually respond to it. Much like the previous steps, you can have a carefully crafted and rehearsed response to each objection style. The trick here is to respond in a way that does not give off a "you're wrong" vibe. Nobody wants to be wrong, even if they are. Think about the last time you were incorrect in an argument. Your first instinct was probably to get instantly angry with not only yourself, but the other person.

That feeling is not ideal if you want the prospect to buy from you, so your best bet is to handle the objection as if it were only a simple misunderstanding. Rather than poking holes in the prospect's objection and trying to shove the facts back in their face, we should only be reminding them that our product/service has the benefits to overcome their objection.

The absolute worst thing you can do here is say anything that can be construed as argumentative, such as the obvious "you're incorrect because…" or even the benign sounding "yeah, but…" Remember, the goal here is not to argue with the prospect, so you have to be careful at this part. Those two phrases (and similar ones) are argumentative because they both imply that the prospect is wrong, and again, nobody wants to be wrong. You might be wondering here, how can we tackle an objection without sounding argumentative?

The best way you can accomplish this is to gently, yet confidently, overcome the objection by playing to both the logical and the emotional side of the brain. Here you want to remind the prospect why this is perfect for them based on both product facts and the *why* behind the product. Facts alone simply won't convince someone to buy after they give an objection. Logic and reason are unexpectedly not good tools for overcoming objections. People simply do not buy for logical reasons, they buy for emotional ones. Pairing the facts with the *why* is how you make it emotional.

Let's go way back to almost the beginning of the road trip. If you remember, our *why* for the security system was that we believe that every family should be safe in their own homes and have the comfort of security. The company seeks to be the preferred provider of security services and uses that *why* as the driving force behind its success. After all, with a *why* like that, what person would want to turn that down? Using this while overcoming the objections with facts is a powerful combination.

Here is how you do it:

> ***Prospect:*** "We are very happy with our current provider and do not want to leave them."
> ***You:*** "I understand what you are feeling. Many people felt the same way when they looked at our services, however, when they tried us out they found that the investment was well worth it. But I just want to make sure we are on the same page here, the reason you are hesitant to try us out is that you feel as if your current provider is sufficiently meeting your needs. Is that all that's preventing you from trying us out?"
> ***Prospect:*** "Yes"
> ***You:*** "**I'm glad that you are taking this seriously and using them. We both have the same goal - to provide you with the comfort of home security. Our standards for that service are higher than most. Because we want to provide you with superior security, our police response rate is more than twice as fast as the other guys. Plus, we provide the mobile monitoring service which, as you said, will be very important for you when you are traveling out of town.**"

In this case, we confidently overcame the objection by reminding them about their needs that they expressed to us and reminded them exactly how our product covers that need. We invoked our *why* again to remind the prospect that our company is concerned about more than just the bottom line - we have a real mission to provide home security to families. If you are sincere about that, the prospect should pick up on that and feel the emotional tug.

Your own objection handling strategies will be different than the ones listed here. It all varies on what you actually sell and what your individual company objection handling strategies are. Overall, your style should follow the same basic formula: logic and facts mixed with your *why*. As you can see from the below examples, all of the methods for overcoming objections sound very similar to each other:

- <u>No need</u>: Well, I just don't think our family needs your security services."
    - o ***Reworded***: "You don't see how our services can benefit your family in a way that is important to you."
    - o ***Overcome Example***: I'm glad that you are taking this matter seriously and looking out for your family. Our mission is to provide families the safety and security that they deserve. We pride ourselves on the fact that we go above and beyond for families like yours. Like we said before, this would be perfect for your family because you do a lot of traveling - we are the leaders in quick response and instant notifications. We designed this for people like you.

- Price: "Honestly, that's out of our budget. Your prices are a little too high for me."
    - **Reworded**: "The product investment is too high for the benefit return you will receive."
    - **Overcome Example**: "I understand - anytime you are looking at a purchasing decision, it's important to weigh the pros and the cons. Here, we strive to be the absolute best provider for safety and security in the area. I believe that the benefits of this package will fit your needs perfectly - the mobile monitoring, the instant notifications, and the quicker than average response are all services that enhance your family safety, which can be invaluable."

- Fear of change: "We are very happy with our current provider and do not want to leave them."
    - **Reworded**: "You feel as if your current provider is sufficiently meeting your needs."
    - **Overcome Example:** "I'm glad that you are taking this seriously and using them. We both have the same goal - to provide you with the comfort of home security. Our standards for that service are higher than most. Because we want to provide you with superior security, our police response rate is more than twice as fast as the other guys. Plus, we provide the mobile monitoring

service which, as you said, will be very important for you when you are traveling out of town."

- <u>Not right now:</u> "That sounds like a good idea, but I have to talk it over with my wife."
    - ○ ***Reworded***: "You are willing to give us a try, but want to confirm your decision with your wife."
    - ○ ***Overcome Example***: "I'm glad that you want to talk to your wife about this. This is a decision that affects the whole family. Here we strive to provide families with everything they need to feel safe and secure. I truly believe that this fits you and your wife's needs perfectly. With you traveling a lot and with our fast response rate and live monitoring services, you can rest easy knowing she will be safe at all times."

- <u>No trust:</u> "I have a hard time believing that I'm going to get all this without some catch."
    - ○ ***Reworded***: "You don't trust that our services can deliver what is being promised."
    - ○ ***Overcome Example***: "First of all, thank you for taking this seriously and looking out for your family. I apologize that I have not effectively communicated our commitment to you. Our goal is to be the best provider of

security services in the area. We want your family to be safe at all times. As shown by the data here, our response rate is statistically far better than the average."

The only thing that differs between the objections is the verbiage, but they all follow the same general guidelines. Once you work to overcome the objection, you can move on to the last part of this stop - closing again.

Repeat the close

A common pitfall that is easy to fall into is to simply be silent after you overcome the objection. This presents the prospect with the opportunity to simply make another objection. The best way you can prevent this from happening is to immediately close again after you tackle the objection.

Revisiting the close might feel strange at first, but remember, the closing strategies are designed to encourage the prospect to say "yes." Using those same closing strategies at this crucial part is the best way that you can increase the possibility of closing the sale. As to which one is best to use here, I believe that there really is no right answer to that question.

I have heard arguments that state that you should always close again with an assumptive-style close. Assuming that the prospect is now fully ready to purchase because you overcame the objection shows confidence. I have also heard arguments that support using any style of close, just as long as it's done properly. Personally, I favor going with the *Assumptive Close*. I feel that it displays the highest level of confidence and trust in the product/service, which as we know, is crucial to closing a sale.

Had we continued with the previous example, the process of closing again would look like:

> *Prospect:* "We are very happy with our current provider and do not want to leave them."
> *You:* "I understand what you are feeling. Many people felt the same way when they looked at our services, however, when they tried us out, they found that the investment was well worth it. But I just want to make sure we are on the same page here - the reason you are hesitant to try us out is that you feel as if your current provider is sufficiently meeting your needs. Is that all that's preventing you from trying us out?"
> *Prospect:* "Yes"
> *You:* "I'm glad that you are taking this seriously and using them. We both have the same goal - to provide you with the comfort of home security. Our standards for that service are higher than most. Because we want to provide you with superior security, our police response rate is more than twice as fast as the other guys. Plus, we provide the mobile monitoring service which, as you said, will be very important for you when you are traveling out of town. **Let's do this: we offer a trial period for 30 days. If you're not satisfied, you are under no obligation to continue with our service. I can start that with the premium package as early as today.**"

At the end of the day, it really doesn't matter what style of close you use. The main point is that you have the courage and the discipline to close again after handling an objection.

Final check

The objection road block, upon first sight, looked pretty daunting and intimidating. A lot of sales people are scared of objections because they believe that they are really difficult to overcome. This is a misconception - objections are indeed hard to overcome...without a strategy. If you have a strategy and a process that you can use to handle every single objection out there, objections suddenly become extremely manageable. Having the ability to 'eat' objections using the I E.A.T. strategy allows you to confidently overcome objections, which greatly increases your opportunity for success.

Before we did any of this, we had already researched common objections, so we know what the proper responses should be. When presented with an objection, all we have to do is follow the process:

> **I**dentify the problem
> **E**mpathize with the prospect
> **A**ffirmation of the problem
> **T**ackle the Objection

After you overcome the objection, you confidently close the prospect again using the method with which you feel most comfortable. At this point in the road trip, you are approaching a three way fork in the road. One of three things is about to happen:

1. You hear a soft "no" from the prospect.
2. You hear a firm "no" from the prospect.
3. You hear a "yes" from the prospect.

If you hear a soft "no," you'll know it. The prospect might say something like "I don't know...I'm still not sure…" This is common for prospects to do. This means that they are teetering on the fence. There might be another minor objection holding them back. If this happens, don't give up. Eat the objection again using the <u>same exact process</u> as before. Go through all the steps - figure out the objection, make sure that's the only concern they have, and then overcome it again. If they answer with another soft "no," do it again! This might sound incredibly awkward, but I once heard a marketing executive go through *four* rounds of objections before closing the prospect. That sale would not have happened if he gave up after the first two rounds. The idea is that anytime you detect any 'wiggle room' with the prospect's rejection, treat it as an opportunity to dig deeper.

The other two ways both lead to the end of our road trip. No matter which way you take, the trip is over. The stakes are pretty high for this one though. To put it bluntly, you either end in success, or end in failure.

Dead End: "No"

"You build on failure. You use it as a stepping stone. Close the door on the past. You don't try to forget the mistakes, but you don't dwell on it. You don't let it have any of your energy, or any of your time, or any of your space." - Johnny Cash, American military veteran and famous country musician

---

At this point, the prospect might give you a hard "no." This is an indication that your road trip is over. Unfortunately, you were not able to get to the final destination. Rather than the prospect buying from you today, they refused to do business with you. You might be wondering - what's the difference between a soft "no" and a hard "no?" As with anything else, the difference is based on a person-to-person basis. While there really is no sure-fire way to know, it's generally safe to assume that the prospect will not buy if they say something along the lines of "Absolutely not. I will not commit to this right now." Deciding that the prospect will refuse to buy is ultimately a situational judgement call on your part. I know that it sounds like poor advice to put it this way, but when the prospect is genuine about not buying, you'll know.

As it stands, the road trip has ended in failure. We did not close the prospect, and therefore, did not make any money for ourselves or for the company. While we did not succeed and get to the final destination, we are still in the car, far away from home. We are still in front of the prospect...we can't just run away. What do we do now?

Understand that this is common

Nobody likes being told "no." As children, we all certainly hated it when our parents told us that we could not do something. As adults, we also hate it when people tell us that something cannot be done. After someone refuses to buy from you, you might have emotions of anger, sadness, frustration, and disappointment. You might even feel a wave of humiliation crash over you, followed by panic. For salespeople, being told "no" can be the worst thing that can happen professionally. It means that we did not do our primary job successfully, so it's a huge blow to the self-esteem.

This happens to everyone

The first thing that you should understand is that this is very common. This happens to every single salesperson on the planet. It does not matter how amazing someone is. It doesn't matter if someone is the number one performer in the company. At some point, everybody ends up here. In most cases, the best salespeople are here the most often! The point being, you are not the first person to fail.

It's also important to realize that this won't be the last time you fail either. Salespeople have to be mentally tough for a reason. It's the reality of our profession. Overall, we will be rejected far more than we will succeed. I once worked in an industry where closing 10% of the prospects that you talked to is considered phenomenal. That means that 90% of the time, professional sales executives are being told "absolutely not." That can be damaging to one's mental state. It takes a lot of mental toughness to keep going when being rejected nine out of ten times.

Do not quit

Not giving up is what separates top performers from those who do not make it. Sometimes it's not that they are better at selling (although that certainly helps), it's that they simply keep going and are not fazed by rejection. A lot of people unfortunately give up before they find success. I have seen naturally talented salespeople quit because they get frustrated. Had they stuck it out a little longer, I am sure they would have been top performers.

A perfect analogy that we can use here is the New England Patriots' comeback in Super Bowl 51 against the Atlanta Falcons. [5]

The Atlanta Falcons were the extreme underdog. The Patriots had the best offense in the NFL and a defense that seemed impossible to breach. Going into the game they were heavily favored. The Falcons came out swinging, though. At halftime everyone was shocked when the Falcons led the Patriots 21-3. The nail seemed to be in the coffin when the Falcons scored again after halftime, making the score 28-3. The game seemed to be over.

In one of the most sensational comebacks ever, the Patriots scored 31 unanswered points and beat the Falcons in overtime. It was something historic in the sports world. Never before had a team come from such a large deficit to win the game, and never before was the game won in overtime.

The obvious lesson here is to never give up. The Patriots were facing some pretty insane odds at the end. They literally had to score twice, get two two-point conversions, win the overtime coin toss, and score on the opening overtime drive. These odds are daunting – even for the Patriots. A lesser team may have simply given up at this point and just wrote the season off as a loss. Not the Patriots.

They did all of the above and won the game in a spectacular fashion. They did not give up; they worked harder to make their dream a reality. For that, they 100% deserve the Super Bowl victory.

You might have some months where you are in a rut. You might be in the middle of a sales call that is going horribly wrong. You might even be on your last warning before losing your job. Regardless of the situation, the only way you will guarantee failure is by giving up. Keep trying and pushing as hard as you can. Believe the impossible.

Keep the sales process open

After you hear the dreaded final "no," your first instinct might be to get out of the conversation as quickly as possible. Why stick around after being rejected? If the prospect refuses to buy, you should get away as quickly as possible so you don't waste any more time, right?

Wrong. What you do after the rejection is ironically as important as anything else on this road trip. Although the prospect is not ready to buy from you right now, the possibility exists that they might be ready in the future. If you accidentally burn the bridge here, the chance of saving the sale later on down the road becomes zero. If you want any chance of saving the sale for a later date, you have to be able to dust off the rejection and leave on good terms with the prospect.

Be respectful

The worst thing that you can do here is express anger or frustration towards the prospect. Remember, the prospect is very defensive at this point. Expressing that you are mad at them for not buying is a great way for the prospect to get upset with you. Think about the last time a salesperson became disrespectful when you did not buy something. It probably left a bad taste in your mouth for the salesperson and for the company. Even if you were going to buy later on, now you are questioning that decision. If this happens in the mind of a prospect, the chance of a prospect buying from you down the line greatly diminishes.

To avoid this from happening, restrain your negative emotions and be respectful towards the prospect. Look them in the eyes, smile, shake their hand, and thank them for their time and for listening. This will certainly be tough to do, but it's important for the prospect to respected and appreciated. In many instances, it can take more than one interaction to close a prospect. During my first sales job post-graduation, you were considered successful if you could close the prospect in under seven interactions. It's important for the prospect to leave this interaction and be OK with seeing you again.

Even if this will be your only interaction with the prospect, the prospect might end up purchasing down the line from someone else within the company. While this does not help your commissions at all, it's still good for the reputation of the company. It also helps your personal reputation as someone who genuinely cares about the success of the team. Sales is competitive, but it's also a group effort. If nobody is selling except for you, the company probably won't be around much longer. Celebrate the wins of teammates and focus on closing your next call.

Being bitter about losing a sale to someone else achieves nothing other than frustration and jealousy. It's important to not only be respectful of prospects, but of coworkers too.

Dust off

Dusting off a rejection can quickly get awkward. Think about all the high school themed comedy movies where a guy gets rejected by a female classmate. Usually, the guy does something cringe worthy and embarrassing as he tries to brush off the rejection. Being rejected is an unpleasant and uncomfortable feeling, so it's only natural to react accordingly. Unfortunately, salespeople really don't get this luxury. They have to dust off rejection with the same confidence as before.

As we already said, part of being respectful is looking them in the eyes, smiling, shaking their hand, and thanking them for their time and for listening. This is a great way to display body language to show that you remain confident in yourself and the product/service. It's not just about what you physically do though - you have to tell the prospect that you understand. You also should tell the prospect that you respect their decision.

- "Mr. Jones, I understand and respect your decision. Thank you for taking the time out of your busy day to listen to me."

Part of the dust off step is keeping the sales process open. If possible, ask the prospect if you can set a future appointment to discuss the matter further; perhaps at that time you will have a new product/service to offer that will fit their needs better. Or you can leave your information with the prospect and request that if they have any further questions to give you a call. Even if the prospect just calls about a simple question, it's still another interaction, which means another chance to sell. The idea is to increase the chance of speaking with the prospect again. Even if it's something as simple as a coffee break! Whatever you can do to get in front of that prospect again will at least give you another chance to close.

- "Mr. Jones, I understand and respect your decision. Thank you for taking the time out of your busy day to listen to me. Here is my card with my number on it. **If you have any questions about anything at all, just give me a call and I'd be happy to help.**"

Once the interaction is done, the road trip is over.

Analyze your trip

The difference between top performers and those who continue to end up here is that the top performers learn from their failed sales calls. Rather than viewing it as an utter failure, they view it as a learning opportunity to get better. Part of getting better is studying your mistakes and working to overcome them before the next call. Do this enough and you will improve.

Look back at every turn you took and every stop that you visited. Examine what you did wrong. Perhaps it was that you rushed through the *Discovering a Need* stop too fast, or maybe it was that you forgot to describe a feature. Whatever it was, take a note of it. Work to avoid that mistake next time you head on another trip. If you do this with every single road trip that you embark on, you'll find that you'll end up at the *Closed Sale* destination more often.

It's not just about analyzing what went wrong. Equally as important, examine where you succeeded. While you should seek to minimize the mistakes that you make, you should also be looking to maximize the wins that you have during the trip. Maybe you were excellent at building rapport or perhaps you gave the perfect pitch. Whatever you did well, celebrate it and look to repeat that behavior next time around.

This is where top performers are made. Those who can improve every single call are the ones who are constantly number one in the office. They take their destiny into their own hands. Failure is something that happens to everyone. Those who are able to withstand it, dust off rejection, keep the sales process open, and learn from their mistakes are the ones who will be extremely successful salespeople.

Final Destination: Closed Sale

"Success is no accident. It is hard work, perseverance, learning, studying, sacrifice, and most of all, love what you are doing or learning to do." - Pelé, Retired Brazilian soccer player, voted World Player of the Century and Athlete of the Century

---

Congratulations! You have made it to the final destination of our road trip: the *Closed Sale*. This is what we have been working towards the entire trip - that moment where the prospect agrees to purchase and officially becomes a customer. Your preparation, your discipline, and your courage have all led you to this moment. This is where you can call yourself a professional salesperson - when you successfully close a deal.

Before we get too ahead of ourselves here, we still have some work to do. Believe it or not, even though the prospect agrees to buy, we still have some final steps to complete before we can legitimize the sale. Hardly ever does someone agree to buy something significant and hand you money right away. A conversation has to be made about the details of the purchase so nothing is missed and so that the prospect fully understands. That's why it's important to lock in the sale.

Lock in the sale

Locking in a sale is not the same thing as closing a sale. When you close, you are trying to get the prospect to say "yes." When you lock in a sale, the prospect has already agreed to buy, so all you have to do is confirm the sale and go over the next steps. It's the final bridge between prospect and customer that needs to be crossed, and luckily, it's one of the easiest bridges to cross.

Validation and reassurance

If the prospect tells you that they agree to purchase, you should not act if you are surprised at their decision. This is much easier said than done, especially early on in your career. I can't speak for all salespeople, but when I was closing my first few deals I was so excited that I almost seemed shocked at their decision. It might not be that big of a deal, but remember, we want to display confidence throughout the entire process. If the prospect agrees to buy, we should act as if it was the correct decision, and any other decision would not make sense. This will help validate the sale for the prospect.

We can do that using the same basic principles found in the *Introduce Yourself* stop. We want to look the prospect in the eye, smile, and (if we are in a position to do so) shake their hand. If you are strictly a phone salesperson, you can still do the exercise - it will make you sound more confident. Remain in control of your non-verbal body language and you'll be just fine.

It's always a great idea to reassure the prospect as well. Telling the prospect that they made a wise decision and that they will be happy with that decision will help reassure the prospect. If the prospect feels like they have made a bad choice, there is a good chance that they will rescind. The best way we can help prevent that is to reassure them that they will be extremely satisfied with our product/service/brand.

> **Prospect:** "Yes, I think you are right. I'll go with the premium package."
> *You:* **"Fantastic. You're going to love it. You made a great decision for you and your family."**

Something as simple as that can make a huge difference. If the prospect feels reassured and validated, they will start to believe that they made a good choice, which is absolutely crucial for the sale to finalize. This is not enough though, we have to actually get a firm commitment.

Get the prospect committed

Much like with every other stop along the way, if we rush through this part we might sabotage ourselves and end up with the prospect backing out or returning the product/service. Locking in the sale is essentially committing the prospect to their decision to buy. This can be done a number of different ways, but don't overthink it. This can be with something as simple as a signature or even a down payment. It's a necessary psychological step that the prospect needs to take so they feel invested in the product/service already. If you don't get the prospect committed right then and there, there is a good chance that they can rescind on the sale, which would mean that this entire road trip was unsuccessful.

Let's illustrate this with two different examples using our previous security systems pitch:

> ***Prospect:*** "Yes, I think you are right. I'll go with the premium package."
> ***You:*** "Fantastic. You're going to love it. You made a great decision for you and your family. **I'll have an agent call you tomorrow to set it up.**

While this might seem ok at first, a lot can happen between now and tomorrow. The prospect can decide that they no longer need your product/service. They can change their mind easily because the final commitment won't be occurring until tomorrow, so in their minds they have one full day to examine their purchase from every angle. In the head of a brand new customer who has a day or more before they are committed, there is still time to cancel. Rather than waiting a day or two to gain a real commitment, gaining it on the spot is far more beneficial.

> ***Prospect:*** "Yes, I think you are right. I'll go with the premium package."
> ***You:*** "Fantastic. You're going to love it. You made a great decision for you and your family. **What I'm going to do now is set you up for installation. Let me grab your signature here and we can get you secured.**"

A bird in the hand is worth more than two in the bush. Get the commitment now to reduce people changing their mind right after you leave. Unfortunately, some prospects will cancel no matter how much commitment they give. The idea here is to dramatically reduce that number.

Review the next steps

Gaining a commitment via signature/down payment/whatever you choose is a great way for the new customer to psychologically take ownership of the product/service that they just purchased. We're not done yet though. Now that the customer has mental ownership, they will surely want to know what the next steps in the purchasing process are.

If several additional steps need to be taken before the customer actually starts to use the product/service, it's important to review what the next steps are so there are no surprises down the road. For example:

> **Prospect:** "Yes, I think you are right. I'll go with the premium package."
> **You:** "Fantastic. You're going to love it. You made a great decision for you and your family. What I'm going to do now is set you up for installation. Let me grab your signature here and we can get you secured."
> *Prospect signs name.*
> **You: "I will take this and process it on our end. You will be receiving a call in the next 24 hours with one of our installation teams. From there, you can choose an installation date/time to fit your schedule. You will receive your first bill one month after the installation date."**

It might not seem like a lot, but if you take someone's money and leave without explaining what the next steps are, they might feel a level of uncertainty. Some people might even feel as if they were scammed. You never want your customers to feel like this, so make sure you accurately describe what will happen next leading up to them receiving the product/service.

If you are selling a product or service that the prospect will use or receive immediately, you should still describe the next steps in terms of what they can now expect in terms of functionality and benefits. For example, let's suppose that we have the ability to install the security system right there on the spot:

> **Prospect:** "Yes, I think you are right. I'll go with the premium package."
> **You:** "Fantastic. You're going to love it. You made a great decision for you and your family. What I'm going to do now is set you up for installation. Let me grab your signature here and we can get you secured."
> *Prospect signs name.*
> **You: "Perfect. I will go ahead and install the system right now so we can get you ready and secured as soon as possible. From here on, the system will be monitoring your property for all the dangers we talked about and you will have a team of professionals ready to help out at a moment's notice. Once I install it, we can download the app on your phone and get it registered for even faster notification. I'll get started now."**

Bottom line is that the more information the new customers have about the post-sale process, the more their mind will be at ease.

<u>Dust off</u>

We are almost done. At this point, we've got everything done to solidify the sale. Once we get that firm commitment from the customer and go over the next steps, all we have to do is dust off the customer. As a paid sales professional who works on commission, time is money. The more prospects that you close, the more money you make. Therefore, it's important to not linger on too long past the close. Having an hour long conversation after a close might be great for rapport building, but prevents you from talking to other prospects.

In most cases, your customers are busy people too. It doesn't matter if they are an individual consumer or the purchasing agent representing a multi-million dollar firm; odds are, they have somewhere else to be or something else to do soon. Dusting off the customer after you make the sale will allow you to respect their time as well. Ultimately, you should have a strategy for ending the sales call on a positive and open note.

Notice that we are not trying to sweep away the prospect like they are dirt. If we immediately say "bye" after we close the sale and walk away like we don't care, the prospect might feel taken advantage of. You did all that work building rapport in the beginning - don't throw it all away by getting out of the conversation quickly/rudely. If done correctly, you should get out of the call soon but leave it open for future calls/follow ups.

If your company allows it or if you are in a situation where this is required, always hand out your information after a sale is made. It's always a good idea to give out your office number or email address. Whichever one is fine - it's entirely up to your personal preference. Make sure the customer knows that they can get in contact with you directly so they can follow up with any questions or potential concerns.

Think of it like this: if the customer has a question about the product/service, wouldn't you rather have them asking you instead of someone else? If they don't have a reliable source of knowledge, they can go to their peers or even your competition and try to figure it out. Customer service departments are a great solution for this, but it's more meaningful coming from you than someone they have never spoken to before. At the end of the day you are still putting your destiny in the hands of someone else. Being in control of the post-sale process is important, and this is how you directly influence it.

The same logic applies for customers who have concerns. If they contact you directly, they trust you enough to handle their concern. If a customer calls with problems, you might have to 're-sell' them and go through the road trip all over again, but at least you have a shot at retaining the customer. Again, customer service associates are highly trained in this as well, but it's more meaningful coming from the person they bought from originally.

- "It was an absolute pleasure. Here is my business card - if you ever have any questions or concerns about anything, please don't hesitate to give me a call."

Coming full circle, the final thing you want to do is incorporate the 3 E's that we first used when we met the prospect. Use your *Energy* to stand/sit up straight, look the customer in the eye, smile, and if you're in a face-to-face role, have a strong handshake. Use your *Excitement* and talk in a higher pitched tone of voice. Use your *Enthusiasm* and finish with a strong goodbye.

- "It was an absolute pleasure. Here is my business card - if you ever have any questions or concerns about anything, please don't hesitate to give me a call. **Mr. Jones, have a great rest of your day."**

The road trip is now over. You made it to the final destination and secured the sale. Congratulations! You have officially just had a successful sales call.

Always be improving

After you arrive at your final destination, you're going to feel like you are on top of the world. You made a sale, helped out a prospect, and made some money. You're going to be excited and thrilled with yourself that you were able to successfully win someone over to your way of thinking. You 'won.' This feeling of accomplishment is called "the thrill of the sale," and rightfully so.

Of course, all this was possible because you were not only persuasive and confident, but you stuck to the road map and completed every stop diligently. You did not take any shortcuts and did not speed through the stops. You overcame the road blocks that tried to end your trip. All in all, you stuck to the process.

Now that you have successfully closed a sale, the trick is to not become a one-sale-wonder. You have to maintain this level of success. Success in sales is not about who is the most convincing person in the room…it's about who is disciplined enough to commit to their sales process and stick with it. I'll bet that if you ask any top performing salesperson if they have a structure that they use every single time, they will say that they do. That's how they maintain their status as a top performer.

Not only do top performing salespeople follow the same sales process every time, but they constantly analyze their entire sales call after the fact. Top performers don't just see opportunity to learn when they fail; they also look for it when they succeed. It's important to look back on the road trip and take note of not only the stops where you were exceptional, but those you can improve on. There is always room for improvement. Once you stop analyzing your sales process after every call, you will start the process of becoming stagnant. That's what leads to sales slumps. Constant evaluation and improvement is what keeps people out of ruts and keeps them performing well.

If you are constantly improving and adapting, your road map might end up looking a little bit different than mine. Remember, this road map is my individual sales process. Other people might have different strategies or tactics. If you learn one lesson from this book, make it that you should have a sales strategy, stick with it, and improve on it.

At the end of the day, if you stick to your sales road map, don't try to take shortcuts, and always look for opportunities to improve, you're going to find the final destination and be a successful salesperson.

A Note from Jason

First of all, I just wanted to say thank you for taking the time to read this book. The purpose of this book is simple: to help people improve their sales tactics to result in more closed sales. I wanted to write a sales book that was insightful and meaningful, yet easy to understand. I sincerely hope that it was as enjoyable for you to read as it was for me to write. I also hope that you found the material to be of good use. If you learned one thing from this book, I'll consider it a success.

If you did find value in reading this book, I have one request. As an independent author and blogger, I ultimately depend on honest reviews of my material from people like you. If you have the time, I would greatly appreciate a review of this book on Amazon.

Thank you, and happy selling!

Sources Noted

[1] "Mission, Vision & Values." The Coca-Cola Company, The Coca-Cola Company, www.cocacolacompany.com/our-company/mission-vision-values.

[2] Ziglar, Zig. Secrets of Closing the Sale. Berkley, 1984

[3] Strohmetz, D. B., Rind, B., Fisher, R. and Lynn, M. (2002), Sweetening the Till: The Use of Candy to Increase Restaurant Tipping1. Journal of Applied Social Psychology, 32: 300–309. doi:10.1111/j.1559-1816.2002.tb00216.x

[4] S., Giles, L., & Tzu, S. (2016). The Art of War. United States: Publisher not identified.

[5] Super Bowl LI - New England Patriots vs. Atlanta Falcons - February 5th, 2017. (n.d.). Retrieved July 01, 2017, from https://www.pro-football-reference.com/boxscores/201702050atl.htm

www.ingramcontent.com/pod-product-compliance
Lightning Source LLC
Chambersburg PA
CBHW050207230526
45470CB00001B/269